ZARA YACOB

ZARA YACOB

A Seventeenth Century Rationalist:
Philosopher of the Rationality
of the Heart

Teodros Kiros

AFRICA WORLD PRESS
TRENTON | LONDON | CAPE TOWN | NAIROBI | ADDIS ABABA | ASMARA | IBADAN | NEW DELHI

AFRICA WORLD PRESS
541 West Ingham Avenue | Suite B
Trenton, New Jersey 08638

Book design: 'Damola Ifaturoti
Cover design: Ashraful Haque

**Cataloging-in-Publication Data is available from Library of
Congress**

ISBN: 1-56902-212-7 (Hardcover)
ISBN: 1-56902-213-5 (Paperback)

Contents

Dedication
I dedicate this book to my partner,
Fantaye Tefera

Acknowledgments

I would like to thank Professor Henry Louis Gates of Harvard University for extending to me the privilege of a Du Bois Fellowship in 2002-2003 during which I finished this book. A special thanks to Anthony Appiah for his extensive comments on the various drafts of the manuscript. Over the years the support of Kwasi Wiredu and Claude Sumner has enabled me to mature as a scholar. Both read and supported my different philosophical essays over the past long years. Paget Henry and Lewis Gordon have also been fierce and compassionate supporters of my philosophical work. Their friendship continues to make my stay at Brown University joyful and productive. May Farhat of Harvard University read and critiqued this book extensively, and I would like to express my deepest thanks to her. My daughter Ruwan provided me with love and humor while I finished the book. A special thanks to the Du Bois fellows of 2002-2003 for commenting on a version of the paper I gave as a Du Bois Fellow. My special thanks to my brilliant students at Brown University and Suffolk University. Finally, thanks to all those who attended a talk on Zara Yacob at the Caribbean Philosophical Association meeting in Barbados this year.

Chapter I
CLASSICAL ETHIOPIAN PHILOSOPHY AND THE MODERNITY OF ZARA YACOB

In the long history of Ethiopian philosophy, there have been two dominant traditions, classical Ethiopian Philosophy and the modern rational philosophy of Zara Yacob. These philosophies move into different directions and draw from different sources. Classical Ethiopian philosophy is a confluence of Greek, Egyptian, Aramaic and Arab sources. Zara Yacob's modern rational philosophy introduces a new tradition to the Ethiopian philosophical landscape. To keep matters in perspective I will briefly summarize the main features of classical Ethiopian philosophy and then move on to articulate the modernity of Zara Yacob.

Classical Ethiopian Philosophy
The Fisalgos, according to Sumner, is a transcription from the Greek *Physiologos*. *The Physiologos* is primarily symbolic of moral values. Various ani-

mals, plants and stones are used as symbols of moral instructions, counsels and a distinctly Ethiopian interpretation of the Bible. There is a discourse that is exceptionally illuminating about humans' duties toward their parents. *The Fisalgos* says, "*Any one who curses father or mother must die*" (Exodus 21:17: *Levictus* 20-9); likewise:

> *The young one of the hipwopas, when their father grows old, pluck off his molting feathers, peck his eyes, keep him in a hot place, welcome him under their wings, feed him, and guard him, as is they were saying to their father: As a reward for having kept us, we shall do likewise to you. And they do so until (these aged birds) are imparted with renewed vitality; they are rejuvenated and are young once more.*[1]

The Book of the Philosophers also uses images in the way that the *Fisalgos* does. In contrast to the *Fisalgos*, *The Book of the Philosophers* is a collection of sayings that illuminate tradition as a source of philosophy and philosophy as orality. Most of the sayings are Ethiopianized interpretations of classical Greek sayings. They are transformed sayings by the Great philosophers: Pythagoras, Plato, and Aristotle, but the meanings retain their Ethiopian roots and cadence. (*They are not merely appropriations, but rather transformed interpretations.*) As Sumner correctly argues, Ethiopians never translate literally: they adopt, modify, add, subtract. A translator always bears a typical Ethiopian stamp.

For the sake of brevity, I will choose three perennial moral categories, *wisdom, moderation,* and *faith* to highlight the concern and occupation of the author of *The Book of the Philosophers* in classical Ethiopian philosophy.

3. Wisdom a wise man said: "Nothing is nobler than the mind. Kings condemn people and the learned condemn the Kings." [3] This particular saying, like many that follow, is very Greek in spirit and most distinctly Platonic and Aristotelian. In the saying, the mind is given a privileged status over the body, including that of Kings, whose body is a symbol of power. The mind is always superior to the body. The wise man does not get fooled and seduced by the power and wealth of kings. Wealth of the mind is preferable to the wealth of the body. The wise person knows the difference.

44 The wise man said, " There are four kinds of men." 44 The person who knows and teaches; this person is a scholar. By asking him, one can learn a great deal. The person who knows but does not teach; She is intelligent. Remember her. The person who does not know but teaches: he is in need of guidance. Teach him and guide him. The person who does not know and does not want to learn: she is a fool. Keep away from her. The wise person knows these four types of persons and the types of knowledge they possess and interacts with them accordingly. The lesson to be learned is that different discourses ought to be drawn from varied sources. We should learn from a scholar. We should never imitate a self-righteous teacher. The ignorant teacher who thinks he knows must be avoided like a disease.

65 One of the wise men said, "Wisdom is not good if the action is not good." 65 For Sumner, the saying teaches us that " *Action is the essence of Wisdom*" and that " *Wisdom springs from man's good nature or good character*" Sumner is quite right when while interpreting the saying he concludes that Ethiopian Philosophy does not separate wisdom and moral goodness, manifested in good action. On this view a person is good only to the extent that her practices reveal it, and not because she thinks she is good.

115 It has been said. " Sorrow is of two kinds. One type is that of conscience: the rational soul becomes sad out of lack of knowledge. The animal soul feels sorry out of lack of food and drink and the like." This saying further illuminates the saying (65) above. Any action that is not watered by practical wisdom is useless; it lacks a moral purpose and those who do not value practical wisdom; do not water their soul. An unwatered soul, exactly like an action that is not informed by practical wisdom, afflicts and contaminates the body and consequently the character of the person.

He replied, *"In the tongue."* The tongue has a privileged locus in classical Ethiopian philosophy. The tongue is regarded as a dangerous instrument of speech. It has destroyed many able persons because they did not know how to regulate it; many wise people.   The wise Solomon was once asked: *"Where is the dwelling place of wisdom?"* he asserted, *"The wise man is he who knows the time, the time to speak and the time to keep quiet, the time to listen and the time to reply. He should listen to the talk of the sages with respect and praise them for their*

4

knowledge…the moral virtue of humility should be manifested in our language as well as our attitude.[2] The tongue reveals us to others. We are always using language. Language is the essence of our humanity. That is why we should speak sparingly and wisely; speech can humanize us if we use it well. We can be dehumanized by our speech, when we are not vigilant to time. The tongue as the vehicle of language should be carefully nurtured. We must at all times know when, how and with whom to speak with. Time is to language as thought is to character.

It has been said "Man becomes lord by four things. They are counseling, purity, Knowledge and Faith"[3] Character is not a natural given. Of course some individuals seem to have been born purely. They are the lucky ones. Others purify their character through counseling. Others learn by imitating those who are born pure. Some others have become purer because of faith in God who has purified them. The wise person as in (44) above knows how to become wise by using any or all the sources.

The wise Pythagoras said, *"If the soul does not conquer the flesh, then the flesh becomes the grave of the soul. When you warn a wicked person, do it tactfully with soft words, so that he does not run away from you and develop a sinful inclination into a habit like eating and drinking"* The battle between the flesh and the soul is an important part of classical Ethiopian philosophy, as it was for Plato and Aristotle. This perennial battle is repeated again and again. Consider the following passage, "Solomon, the son of David said, drinking wine with excess is the destruction of many. *"Wine causes the storm of evil" He repeats, "Drinking wine with excess harms and sickens.... My son when you drink wine you must not talk too much, but praise God and give thanks to him. Saying good things while drinking wine is like a precious stone of high value, a pearl alloyed with Gold."[4]* A wise and honorable man avoids evil words and reveals what is in his heart.

The second passage is considerably milder than the first. The self is tactfully advised not to abstain but to enjoy the objects of desire moderately; it does not say deprive the body of desire. Regulate desire through self-control. Pay attention to the dangers of excess, the dangers of unregulated quantity. On this second milder view, the desire of the body is burdensome only to those who have not mastered the technique of self-control. Existence is intimate, precious and private. It must be cherished. Philosophers, kings and others cannot live for those who do not know how to live well. One cannot live for another. One must live for oneself. Learning how to live well, however, requires that we master the technique of mastering desire, which itself is an exercise in self-government.

Faith is one of the lord's of existence. A few wise sayings illustrate the importance of faith in Ethiopia's philosophical and theological topography. The wise say, *"Religion and the king are equal. One is not greater than the other. Religion is for the faithful and the king is its keeper. He who has no faith is vain, and he who has no keeper disappears. He is respected whose faith is just, whose living is good to the very end, who honors his fellow man. His conscience and patience are the sources of his respect,*

*his purity is his protector, and his speech and his equa-
nimity are his rank."* [5] Sumner is very convincing
when he writes, " Wisdom has come out of the
mouth of God, whose name covers all the earth
like a cloud. Human temporal wisdom not only
springs from eternal origin, it also leads to an eternal glory at the end of man's presence in the world,"
and furthermore, " *Wisdom is the foundation of faith,
which renders to the Creator the glory he deserves.
Its head and crown are the fear of God."* [6]

Skendes

The story of Skendes (the Greek Secundis) is a
much-celebrated work that has occupied the fer-
tile imaginations of Greek, Syrian, Arabic and
Ethiopian scholars over the centuries. The Ethiopian text is based on the Arabic, although some
scholars contend that it is stylized on the Greek.
The Ethiopian version recalls the story of Skendes,
who was the son of sagacious parents, who decided to send him to Berytus (modern Beirut) and
Athens for classical education. Skendes was thir-
teen years old at the time of his departure to the
foreign lands. While he was abroad, he was ex-
posed to a statement of the wise philosophers that
said, *"All women are prostitutes".* Needless to say
he was perturbed by the statement and was determined to verify it. After staying abroad for twenty-
four years he returned to his homeland. He re-
called that disturbing statement about the nature
of women and decided to test his own mother.
Through the services of a maidservant whom he
met at a public well, he managed to trick the maid

into letting him into his mother's house to spend the night with her mistress in exchange for one-hundred diners. So he spent the night with his own mother. In the morning he revealed himself to his mother as her very own son. Shocked by the discovery, she hung herself.

Skendes regretted his speech. He condemned his tongue that uncontrolled tongue which spoke in the name of truth and that incurred the death of his mother. He mused that he should not have spoken at all. From that moment on, he became permanently silent. During those days Andryanos was the emperor. The emperor heard the extraordinary story and invited Skendes to his court. When Skendes was ordered to speak, he refused. Instead he wrote his thoughts, and the king also communicated with him through writing. His responses were organized into two sections, with fifty-five questions in the first, and one hundred eight questions in the second. The philosopher developed systematic theories about the essence of God, the angels, man, the world, the sun, the moon, the earth, the stars, the sky, the clouds, the mind, the spirit, the winds, thunder, the air, water, the ocean, the soul, man and woman. Many other discourses speculate on the emotions (peace, anger, hatred, cursing, weeping, sadness, laughter) death, sleep and pleasure. After the emperor carefully listened to his outstanding discourses, he was deeply impressed and did not order the philosopher to speak. Instead it was officially decided that Skendes be treated as a national treasure and be preserved in the priests' archives.

According to Sumner, the obstinate silence

of Skendes, the permanently silent, produced an implacable discourse of speech and silence in classical Ethiopian philosophy. The pervasive philosophy of wisdom through silence, the need to control the tongue, discourse on the nature of women, the miseries, slayings, excess and abstention of desire, fear and anger, which Skendes delicately analyzed, became powerful ethical and septennial themes in classical Ethiopian philosophy. The following propositions below are typical representatives of the second section with one hundred eight questions.

If lust is a law that God made to build the world. (385) (1)

Death teaches men a lesson so that they may fear. (387)(15)

You will not take with you anything but your own good works. (385)(4)

Speaking about God leads to wisdom. (393)(6)

If you possess all wisdom, then silence is the highest of all. (393)(12)

I will now select a few statements from classical Ethiopian philosophy, which I think

are illuminating

[Question 20]

Skendes was asked: *"What is mind?"*

He answered: *"The mind is a hidden good; it is the light of the soul, a fire producing many thoughts; it accomplishes actions; it commands language; it is rational; it controls thoughts; it creates secret actions; it feeds and strengthens intelligence; it is the honor of the body; the adornment of wisdom; setting it up rightly"* (186)

[Question 108]

The philosopher was asked: *"Which part of our body is the most evil? And which is easier to control so that man may be saved?"*
He replied:

> *There are many gates in man that bring and draw him to all that is [evil]. Man did not close the gates of the openings that brought the evil waters to him. The other gates can be closed. Many evil ideas come through hearing. The power of sight cannot overcome what is heard. For what is heard overwhelms what the heart thinks. The hand touches, the tongue speaks. But all these senses are overcome by the power of hearing; all the rest would obey you.* (223).

The philosophy of Zara Yacob is clearly and definitely a major departure from the above sapiential themes of the *Book of the Philosophers, Fisalgos'* and *Skendes'* sayings. At issue is not the status of the thoughts. They are broadly speaking philosophical in their own right. It is the case, however, that they are derivative transformations of non-Ethiopian texts to which Skendes and many others contributed. Some of the sayings are natively Ethiopian, based on observation, reports, readings of the Bible and other unknown sources. Given Ethiopia's location and history, as the original home of the species and a major trading center, it is not an accident that the sapiential themes at once are Arabic, Syrian, Biblical and Greek. Ethiopia is clearly a confluence of world cultures. Its philosophical tradition precisely reflects that confluence.

These philosophical reflections are interesting in several senses. To begin with these ethical counsels, as derivative as they are, become transformed by Ethiopian thinkers into much more than their original form. The various traditions, customs, examples and religious belief systems impose themselves on the original forms and radically alter them. This does not mean that just because they have been ethiopianized they have therefore become superior. That is not the point; in certain cases one does hope that they had actually retained their originality. Their adopted meanings are actually more oppressive, backward and blatantly reactionary in certain cases. In spite of these noted weaknesses, they are distinctly Ethiopian, and we must cherish them in their own right.

Furthermore, these sayings give us a novel opportunity to closely inspect the meaning of tradition in the Ethiopian context. After we fully engage ourselves with these traditions and customs that we can position ourselves to appreciate the criticality and originality of Zara Yacob, an individual who was born to this society, and who somehow managed to transcend the limitations of his time, emerging as the first rationalist and modernist, and who simultaneously appropriated and transcended the sapiential tradition that engulfed him. Sumner writes, *"One may query to what extent a work translated from an Arabic text which goes back to a Greek original can be called Ethiopian."* The answer is that this work of translation,

the same could be said of the original works of
Zara Yacob and of Walda Heywat is Ethiopian,
not by the originality of its invention, but by the
originality of its style. Ethiopians never translate
literally; they adapt, modify, add, subtract. A translation therefore bears a typically Ethiopian stamp:
although the nucleus of what is translated is foreign to Ethiopia, the way it is assimilated and
transformed into an indigenous reality is typically
Ethiopian. To illustrate his point he reports about
a particular case of translation. He writes:

> *One example taken from The Book of
> the Philosophers will suffice to drive this
> point home. The well-known conversa-
> tion between Diogenes and Alexander
> of Corinth, which is recorded by Diogenes
> Laertius, is found in our Ethiopian
> work. But it is transformed beyond rec-
> ognition. "Move away from my shadow"
> of Diogenes is ascribed to Socrates in
> Ethiopic, as it already was in the Ara-
> bic. The whole passage has been given
> such a specifically Christian form and
> development that one seems to be listen-
> ing to an Oriental monk speaking
> through the mouth of Socrates. Alexander
> the Great is simply called "The King"-
> and the Arabic does as well. As in most
> other passages in our manuscript, he is
> placed in an inferior position in relation
> to the wise man. The whole dialogue
> hinges around one point: life. For Socrates
> the real life is the spiritual one. But the
> king misses the point, and thinks that
> Socrates is speaking of the temporal life.*[7]

There are many such instances of appropriation and transformation, which are different from Zara Yacob's interpretation and transcendence, which I will examine later. Consider the following saying that is attributed to Plato and typically it is unreferenced.

> *It happened that Plato was ordering young men to be pure and was advising them to hold their tongue and to keep silence."* They said: *"How can one have friends"* He said, *"By respecting them when they are with him and by keeping good memory of them when they are away.* [8]

It is a very wise counsel; it is useful. One can learn from it how to maintain friends by practicing the advice. Perhaps Plato actually said it, or may be he did not, at least not exactly that way. May be he said something else entirely different. The Ethiopian reader does not know. She is simply instructed through a translation of a foreign thinker from another culture. The translator assumes authority. Worse still, the translator uses the name of a major philosophical name to transpose his wisdom, to sound convincing. The writer subtly imposes on Plato's universe, the reader is simply brainwashed. He has not read the texts, is not familiar with the context of the writing. Unfortunately, this is how wisdom was spread at the time. That is how traditions originated and entrenched themselves. This is a classic example of the workings of ideological hegemony. [9]

Another example. A wise man said: *"A reasonable person knows his fellow man and takes care of his own self. He holds his tongue. What is most important in conscience is faith, fear of God, good behavior towards all, love of one's brother."*[10] Here again, short of reference, the reader would not know whether this is an appropriation, an original invention or interpretation. As an Ethiopian reader and professional philosopher, I am tempted to think that the statement sounds distinctly Ethiopian. The statement is clearly said by a Christian thinker, a believer in general. Any ordinary Ethiopian would find that statement coherent, understandable and something that one could strive for. One has to be a believer, however, to be swayed by it, to accept it. The premises are peculiarly that of a religious society, at least on the surface. The wise man manages to blend reason with faith, particularly the fear of God, since the Bible says, the fear of God is the beginning of knowledge. In short, the statement is an Ethiopian invention. If we knew more, if we at least had access to a name of a known person, as we did with Plato, we will be in a better position not to so hastily conclude that it is distinctly Ethiopian. Since the statement does invoke an authority, it is safe to conclude that this is a smart ethical statement that provokes thought and seeks to give us a vision of a reasonable person. The statement qualifies as sapiential and ethical. It is simple and elegant, and convincing because of that. Any illiterate but spiritually alert Ethiopian could understand it. The statement is truly useful counsel to an Ethiopian who encounters the thought either

in Ge'ez or in Amharic and Tigrigna, two dominant Ethiopian national languages.

The following statements ring with the voice
of convention,

110 The wise man *said*, "*Do not reveal your wealth
to your relative and to your sons, for if they see the
abundance of your wealth they will wish for your
death, or if they realize that your wealth is small,
they will look down upon you*" and "*Do not reveal
your love to your lover, so that she will not be elated.*"

111 It *has been said*, "*He who respects the others
will not be humiliated. Three things will increase
respect and honor in a child. They are: obeying the
father, respecting his guests and receiving them with
a pleasant face, and keeping knowledge*"[11]

I will conclude with the following statement
that speaks to us through the voice of Ethiopian
tradition.

112 *A wise man said*, "*A man who passes from foolishness to wisdom is strong indeed.*"

They said to one of the sick people: "*What do you
want?*" He replied, "*I want to be saved from my
sin, for it is because of this that I am sick.*"

A wise man said to a sick person, "*Do you want us
to call for a physician?*" He replied, "*It is a physician
who made me sick!*"[12]

All three statements are razor sharp, ironic,
biting and cynical, and deeply rooted in local tradition.

The first statement is peculiar to Ethiopian
life. The average Ethiopian is distrustful, suspicious to a fault, cynical about human motives, including his own children. A typical Ethiopian is

advised not to show off wealth, clothing and even good looks, or else the evil eye will strike him. The rule of the thumb is to be understated, enigmatic, and inconspicuous and falsely humble. The wise man's advice is steeped in this specific tradition.

To a significant extent statement 111 is an original, although traditional societies such as China are also acutely sensitive to the status of the elderly. This is particularly true of Confucius, whose ethical principles have high regard for the place of parents and the elderly. The Ethiopian ethical principle motivates children to respect their elders so these children too can expect similar respect when they get old. The same applies to respect for guests and keeping knowledge. The starting point is always you, the doer. Do not do to others what you do not want others to do to you. Kindness will be reciprocated with kindness, cruelty with cruelty. So one is advised by the wise to keep this possibility in mind. The advice in these statements is strategic, some might even say opportunistic. The counselor is a pragmatist and a politician. Like Machiavelli, in *The Prince*, the counselor is revealing to others, the road to success and the avoidance of disappointment with the actions of those whom we antagonize, because we do not how to regulate our behavior. We are given strategic lessons with ethical consequences, and not simply ethical principles without consequences.

The last two statements are classical exercises in Ethiopian cynicism. The last one in particular is marred by suspicion, including distrust of medical knowledge. No one knows anything, except

16

oneself. I have dealt with Classical Ethiopian philosophy at such length because of the following reasons.

First, Classical Ethiopian Philosophy is a model of Philosophy in a very broad sense, and I wanted to create a place for that kind of philosophy that marks an emerging sub discipline as part of philosophy in Africa. I think Sumner and now me, present the material in this new way.

Second, I wanted to present this broadly gagged philosophy as a brand of tradition, a tradition that is simultaneously appropriative and transformative. This kind of philosophy adopts, transliterates, adds, subtracts, and in this sense transforms the values and traditions that it willingly embraces, but does so in a novel way. Nothing that comes from outside is accepted on face value. It is fundamentally changed.

I now want to argue that after we fully understand this tradition that we cannot help but become deeply impressed by the rise of Zara Yacob and Walda Heywat, as extraordinary intelligences who transformed to a higher level the transformed tradition that was readily available to them, to which they were born. They did not merely appropriate, they interpreted and transcended their own interpretations. Zara Yacob, who was the more radical and critical of the two, introduced two hitherto unknown methods of interpretation, *Hassasa* and *Hatata*, and revolutionized the field of philosophy in Ethiopia. Sumner is right when he contended that Zara Yacob along with Descartes was a founder of modern philosophy, to which I add that Zara Yacob and Walda Heywat are the first rationalists and modernists in Ethiopian history.

Now that I have laid the groundwork I am in a position to distinguish modernity and tradition, and present the content of Zara Jacob's modernity in full. I would like to begin with a passage that beautifully starts with a juxtaposition of tradition and modernity by Kwame Gyekye:

> *It may be said that from the point of view of a deep and fundamental conception of tradition, every society in our modern world is "traditional" in as much as it maintains and cherishes values, practices, outlooks, and institutions bequeathed to it by previous generations and all or much of which on normative grounds it takes pride in, boasts of, and builds on [...] modernity is not always a rejection of the past. The modern is characterized as scientific, innovative, future oriented, culturally dynamic, and industrialized and urbanized.*[13]

This definition is good as far it goes. The definition accurately characterizes modernity, and further more, it convinces us to see the interface between tradition and modernity. It is very useful way of looking at the topography of society and its dynamic institutions. But it does very little to help us understand the project of the lone philosopher who must sometimes breakaway completely from the past in order to propel society itself to move forward precisely because of an originally philosophical vision and program. The modernity of a philosopher is radically different from the modernity of society, or so it should be, I argue. In this highly qualified sense, the modernity of Zara Yacob is a rejection of tradition, where the values of Ethiopian tradition were found to be unacceptable by reasonable standards, the standard of rationality. He does not simply appropriate traditions from outside, nor, does he bow down to the customs of the society into which he is born, and obviously not by choice, but by the accidents of birth and history. How can one accept something just because he is born into it? Least of all, the philosopher, whose entire task is critique, detachment and constant and dynamic change, which he must practice all the way until his final days.

Philosophy is a critical moral activity. Zara Yacob's rationality used philosophy as a critical/rational activity. There is no extant traditional value that was not severely criticized. His views of faith, of women, of marriage, the care of the body, equality, and human nature are truly revolutionary and genuinely modern for his time. For the rest of the chapter I will engage the above value topics and the refreshing modernity that enveloped them. He was brave and honest to openly avow his devotion to God, and declare his disappointment with the nature of men, whom he found to be unreliable, unwise, sluggish and liars[14]. He did not single out Europeans for these merciless assaults, but the individuals of his homeland- whom he met during his lifetime. He did not take the customary route of singling out the Frang for attack and his countrymen for undeserved adulations or cowardly indifference to their practices. He did not spare any one from rationality's scrutiny. His rationality of the heart continues a critical discourse first displayed in the prose of Sophocles' *Antigone,* where the authority of tradition was challenged by Antigone, a heroine of rationality, who used her intelligence and became determined to dismantle an unreasonable law that forbade her to bury her brother, who had challenged Athenian laws and was killed for it. Zara Yacob, continues this heroic tradition, heroism, humbled by a passion for God, the fountain of wisdom. He prayed to God to make him intelligent and wise so as to use reason accurately and fairly and decipher human nature and inform it with moral wisdom and depth. This was the first test of Rationality.

He could not withstand some traditional absurdities pertaining to the care of the body. His modernity here was eloquent and once again brave and self-confident. Some of the laws of Moses are absurd according to Zara Yacob. It is absurd for example, to condemn marriage as evil as Moses did. Marriage is a natural activity to fulfill the human need for propagating children and for sustained companionship of other human beings. Marriage gives both things at the same time. He argues, " *our intelligence tells us and confirms to us without proof that marriage springs from the law of the creator; and yet monastic law renders this wisdom of the creator ineffectual, since it prevents the generation of children and extinguishes mankind.*"[15] So is the doctrine of Mohammed marred by absurdity? Polygamy is not fair; It violates the rights of men and women. He observed,

> *Those who will be born both male and
> female are equal in number; if we count
> men and women living in an area, we
> find as many women as men; we do not
> find eight or ten women for every man;
> for the law of creation orders one man to
> marry one woman. If one man marries
> ten women, then nine men will be with-
> out wives.*[16]

The creator of fairness could not possibly con-
done this unfair practice. I will leave a final judgment of the argument for later. The absurdities of
Moses are even more glaring when it does come
to his judgment of a woman's capacity, as for example, when Moses teaches us that anything a
woman touches is impure because of the blood
that flows from her. This blood flows for a reason;
it is instrumental to the generation of children. If
that is the case, how can we condemn a woman
for this impurity, and prevent her from touching
anything because she is so dirty? This flawed logic
emanates from man who is inherently flawed. It
could not originate in the creator, the source of all
intelligence and wisdom. The creator knows the
purpose for which this particular female function
was designed. He cannot possibly condemn his
created creature for a task that she performs.
Moses had it wrong. But a generation of believers
was raised believing in falsity. Furthermore, " Likewise the Mohammedans said that it is right to go
and buy a man as if he were an animal. But with
our intelligence we understand that this Moham-
medan law cannot come from the creator of man

who made us equal, like brothers, so that we call our creator our father. But Mohammed made the weaker man the possession of the stronger and equated a rational creature with irrational animals; can this depravity be attributed to God?" [17]Rationality critiques tradition here so powerfully. The answer is no. The tradition is a man made oppressive system. Zara Yacob -the rationalist knew that, and was out to demolish the argument that had been cemented in years and years of tradition and expertly power. Expertly power garbed under the rubric of scientific rationality is powerfully critiqued by the rationality of the heart. The Mohammedans are using rationality in a discriminatory way, and this is in complete violation of God's doctrine, which states that, " discrimination cannot exist in the sight of God, who is perfect in all his works" [18]

The body was handled with remarkable perspicacity by Zara Yacob's modernistic gaze. He was committed to the argument that God never orders absurdities. He does not order us to eat this kind of food today, and another kind of food the next day; nor does he order us not to eat meat but only vegetables. He certainly does not order us to deprive our body of food, sex and drink. He could not have possibly ordered the Mohammedans to eat at night but not during the day. All these orders are absurd and unreasonable. God knows that we traumatize the body by depriving it of food. Food is the creator's gift to us, for which he expects us only to thank him. So is sexual attraction. Sex is also the creator's gift to us. His only demand is that the sexual intercourse has to be legitimate. We are also expected not to indulge in any of his gifts to us. Moderation is the rule of rationality.[19]

For seventeenth century Ethiopia, Zara Yacob's views on gender equality were truly enlightened and extremely progressive. He adored his wife. His respect of her is fully manifest in an eloquent passage that I quoted earlier, where he writes,

> *There was a certain maidservant of my master whose name was Hirut; she was not beautiful, but she was good natured, intelligent and patient. I said to my master Habtu: Give me this woman as a wife. My master Habtu agreed and told me. "Hereafter she is not my maidservant, but yours." But I replied: "I do not wish her to be my maidservant but my wife; husband and wife are equal in marriage; we should not call them master and maidservant; for they are one flesh and one life... this Hirut loved me greatly and was very happy. Formerly she was looked down upon in the house of Habtu, and men in the house made her suffer. But since she loved me so, I took the decision in my heart to please her as much as I could, and I do not think there is another marriage which is so full of love and blessed as ours.*[20]

Needless to say, these are extraordinary statements. The philosopher subtly introduces us to a new philosophy of love. His notion of beauty is not carnal and superficial. It is not based on body structure or class privilege. Good nature, patience and intelligence are his cardinal virtues. They are the sediments of beauty. Physical appearance is a travesty. Most importantly woman is the equal of man, made of the same flesh and for life, a life of respect and equality. His concern about women extends to their sexual rights. He writes, " He who abandons his wife abandons her to adultery and thus violates the order of creation and the laws of nature."[21] Again, his view is extraordinary in that he does not preach what was customary then—that women have no business to think of themselves as sexual beings, and that they should put up or shut up. He dared to challenge this ideology, very much along our modern feminist language. He was the first to think about women's rights in modern Ethiopia, perhaps even in the world.

His sustained reflections on Faith are unusual as philosophical discourses. They are original blends of religious convictions disciplined by thought. Many modern philosophers would dismiss off hand as not philosophical. Zara Yacob proudly and explicitly invokes God's name at every juncture of his meditations. His fundamental conviction is that God exists. Not for a moment does he cast an iota of doubt that God is the creator of everything that is and of everything that will be. His faith is profound and powerful and nothing could change that faith. That is the beginning of his thought. Everything he says in the *Treatise* hinges on that. It is the centerpiece of his metaphysics and moral philosophy. Given that faith, he proceeds to make that faith rational. It is that project that makes his philosophy rational, and rationality is an attribute of modern Philosophy.

He is the first African philosopher who consistently argued that God is not only an object of faith. That would trivialize the meaning of God, if God means anything at all. He believed that God is rational, purposeful and powerful. He created humans who are born with an intelligence that they ought to use to partake in the rationality, purposefulness and power of their creator. The creator made sure that his children are born in His image. He created us as rational creatures that are intelligent and equal. We were all born for birth, peace, love, and death. He is the God of the universe. If we so wish, we can imagine this Rational God mentally. We can imagine him, as immortal, who in turn has endowed us with the capacity for immortality. You can look for Him. You can meditate about him. If the search and the meditation are sincere, he will reveal His rational wisdom to you. To be a beneficiary of this divine dispensation demands from you that you have faith in this Transcendental being. His advice is unfailingly rational. But His ways are mysterious. They will not be readily comprehensible to you. The rational person encounters this challenge with the understanding that she will not immediately comprehend the inner architectonic of faith. For Zara Yacob, true faith is always rational. It cannot withstand irrationality. Irrational actions occur because humans follow their own flawed rationality by mistaking it with God's rationality. If one successfully follows God's doctrine, ones actions become rational, when one does not, the actions are almost always irrational. On this view rationality is not a given, what are given are intelligence and will, and it is the proper use of both that makes it possible for us to develop a rational way of life, as a habitual style of existence. That possibility, Zara Yacob instructs, is found upon a heartfelt belief in the existence of a creator. For Aristotle before Zara Yacob any human action is incomplete without the participation of reason, to which Zara Yacob added that God must inform human action. Aristotle's prime mover is Zara Yacob's God. That is how far the similarities go.

Finally, Zara Yacob's notions of human nature are arrestingly modern. He, like Machiavelli before him, is a shrewd observer of human behavior. He is critical, sufficiently suspicious, and cautiously optimistic. He does not unnecessarily expect much from us humans. Nor does he damn us, like Hobbes before him that we are nasty and brutish. He has a balanced view of our capacities. As I have already argued above when we use our intelligence to the fullest, undistracted by the swings of emotion, and most particularly, when we listen to the inner voice of reason, as Quakers rightly assert, no one can doubt our capability of constructing just social institutions run by rational rulers. But that has not occurred very frequently in human history, precisely because we miserably fail to tap into this source, where God is present. The capacity to uncover the hidden treasures of rationality require an exceptionally strong will, and it is the very lack of this will that defeats most humans. Our will power in comparison to our intelligence is very weak. Many possibilities have been missed not because we lack in intelligence, but importantly because we are weak and sluggish, prone to refuse to sincerely know ourselves.

We are so weak that we cannot look at ourselves in the mirror we instead prefer to lay; we hide behind a mask. If we can, we would not mind eliminating those who really know who we are, if what they expose about our nature is not flattering. We choose lies over truths, flattery over criticism, vanity over modesty. We like to think that we already know, by mistaking what has been passed on to us in the form of tradition, as knowledge that we originated. This dangerous habit infuriates, Zara Yacob. It is precisely this cast of mind, this ideology that led him to conclude that human beings would have to be hopelessly lazy to thoughtlessly make their own what they did not construct. How could any human being refuse to choose for herself, when she has been endowed with the power to think for herself? The philosopher sadly realizes that human beings prefer the comfort of tradition to the agony and uncertainty of knowledge. This frustration, however, does not compel him, as it did the passionate modernist Rousseau after him, to force human beings to be free. Unlike Rousseau and many other scientific rationalists of our time, he solitarily despaired about the human condition, and left redemption to be a transcendental task- a power he believed was reserved for God. Not once in the *Treatise* does he seek to change others. Hubris and vanity did not tempt him. He concentrates solely on his soul, praying that others choose, that path of thought, that thread of solitude and prayer, that daily conversation with the loving and generous redeemer of souls. He writes:

> *And when in the Psalter of David I encounter things that do not agree with my thought, I interpret them and I try to make them agree with my science [emphasis mine] and all is well. While praying in this manner, my trust in God grew stronger. And I said: "God hear my prayer, do not hide from my petition. Save me from the violence of men. For your part, Lord, do not withhold your kindness from me. May your love and faithfulness constantly preserve me. I invoke you O' Lord, do not let me be disgraced. Turn to me and pity me. Give me your strength, your saving help, to me your servant, this son of a pious mother, give me one proof of your goodness…guide me…lead me… Rescue me from my persecutors, for the goodness you show me…do not let me fall into the hands of my enemies… I was praying day and night with all my heart this and other similar prayers.*[22]

In this passage and many others, what is striking is the philosophical quality of the prayers themselves. Many able philosophers do not philosophize through prayers. Whereas that is exactly what Zara Yacob did with and to prayers. He made prayers vehicles of philosophical communication.

He argues through them. They are the propositions of language transposed to the domain of the transcendental dwelling place. Just like Socrates consulted the oracle at Delphi, Zara Yacob attempted to reach the height of the heavens to converse with God.

Chapter II
ETHIOPIA IN THE SEVENTEENTH CENTURY
The Jesuits' perception of Seventeenth Century Ethiopia

Zara Jacob's Ethiopia in the seventeenth century attracted conflicting images. It was the focus of numerous fantasies. Explorers and evangelists were drawn to it, and others constructed diverse myths about the place. According to Lobo, for Ethiopians, their empire began with Adam and continued with Facilidas.[23] But in contrast, the dominant view of the Portuguese Jesuits was shamelessly provincial and chauvinistic. A typical view held that, *"the light of the Gospel, however, having come into the world, also reached and illuminated the Abyssinian people who were living in the dark shadow of paganism"*[24]

The modern nation of Ethiopia is a synthesis of a mosaic of civilizations. A variety of ethnic, linguistic and religious groups came to form this historically rich region. It is said that the earliest settlers of the area, the Sabaeans came from Southwest Arabia, in the first millennium B.C.

and brought with them a sophisticated Semitic speech, writing and elaborate stone-building tradition. Geez is the prominent language that emerged out of this interaction. The famous civilization in Axum seems to have benefited from their presence. It was Ezana, an Akusmite King, who accepted Christianity in the mid-fourth century, which was used to forge a powerful Christian empire under a centralized rule. The Ethiopian Orthodox Church is a product of the Christian empire state. However the rise of Islam in the eight-century introduces tension in the area. The diffusion of Islam creates a rivalry between Christians and Muslims. Threatened Ethiopian Emperors appealed to a European power, such as Portugal, to contain the rise of Islam. The Amhara highlanders and the Northern Tigreans, two dominant linguistic groups made frequent attempts to squelch the Muslim dwellers of the Red Sea and the Gulf of Eden. These skirmishes reached their height when the Amharas and the Tigreans faced a ferocious Muslim advance in the midsixteenth century. At that point the Portuguese arrive on the scene to spread Catholicism, through the mediation of the Jesuits. As events unfold the Portuguese presence turned to be of a mixed blessing.

Ethiopian politics in the seventeenth century was dominated by a powerful wind blowing from the military ambitions of Imam Ahmad ibn Ibrahim al Ghazi, popularly known as Ahmed Gragn to the Ethiopian public. Immediately after Gragn ordered the Muslim town of Adal not to pay its tributes to then emperor of Ethiopia, Emperor Lebna Dengel, Gragn defeated the emperor's army at the battle of ad-Dir in 1527. Lebna Dengel essentially became a fugitive after this major military blow. Soon, his son Galawdewos took over after his father's death in 1540 (Prouty and Rosenfield, 101-2).

This defeat caused Lebna Dengel, before his death to seek help from Portugal to contain Muslim ambitions. In February 1541, 400 well-equipped musketeers led by Dom Christovo de Gama arrived in Massawa. He combined his forces with Empress Sebla Wangel and the Tigrean Army in April of 1542, and forced Gragn to retire in the Tana area. But with the help of a Turkish Army Gragn returned and beheaded Dom Christovo. Sooner, did Ghelawdewos managed to defeat Gragn and killed him in battle. This victory did restore the pride of a wounded nation and brought temporary respite from the savagery of war and pestilence for fourteen years.

Zara Yacob was living during these turbulent times. His Ethiopia was religiously torn between Christianity and Islam. As if that was not enough the intrusion of the Catholic faith to the country disturbed even more the topography of the country. The Portugese presence also came with tremendous arrogance, which infuriated the philosopher and led to speak his mind to his compatriots, some of whom betrayed and put him at loggerheads with the Jesuits.

While Ethiopians were taught that they were living in the center of the universe, the birthplace of Christianity, the Portuguese convinced themselves that Ethiopians needed an authentic Christian credo since the Gospels did not sprout in Ethiopia. At the very least what we witness in this original encounter is a classic cultural hostility and arrogance of two ancient civilizations: Ethiopia and Portugal. According to F.Rez, the Portuguese presence in 17th century Ethiopia resulted in *"throwing back the country into deeper isolation and prolonging the period of its aloofness from the world-besides implanting in the minds of the people seeds of suspicion of our foreign enterprise, religious and other seeds which bear the fruit even today. Even today the gates of Abyssinia cannot be said to be very widely open."*[25] Ethiopia closes itself to any foreign penetration and this fact remains true for the twentieth century.

All the relevant authors of the time concur that the Jesuitical perception of Ethiopia was marred by profound prejudice. Lobo insisted on creating dangerous distinctions among an already divided language groups within Ethiopia. Witness the following divisive statement:

> *The Amharas are the best people, the most courteous and the most pleasant to deal with; the most numerous are the Gallas, all of whom are Pagan. They are barbarous and ferocious, foreigners to the land, having appeared... they came from the interior of Africa in countless numbers destroying Kingdoms and provinces throughout... all Ethiopia is being filled with Ants* [26]

Lavishing on their rapacious appetite, the author added,

This is the land where honey and butter flow [27]

The Portuguese perception of Ethiopia, however, was not monolithic. It varied from Jesuit to Jesuit. Whereas Mendez was persistently disrespectful, Paez was unusually respectful and open-minded. Prutsky, loudly declaring prejudices, reminiscent of Mendez's habits, wrote,

> *Ethiopians are manner less, desire runs unchecked, and passions rise without restraint, instinct rules reason* [28]

Like the luminous Ricci, who endeared himself through his impeccable generosity, Paez was affable and loved by Ethiopians. Paez admired the large and beautiful eyes of Zera Dengel, the Ethiopian Emperor, whom he described as manly and tall, with thin lips and "color unbecoming in Europe". He admired, Susyenos, the Ethiopian emperor who converted to Catholicism and described him as *"virtuous, and [he] combines firmness with prudence, justice with mercy; he loves peace, punishes dissidents and trouble makers, is sparing of wine uncommon among Ethiopians and is also very intelligent"* [29]

Just as Ricci showed the Chinese how to read clocks, Paez displayed musical and mathematical instruments, and taught the Ethiopians how to hew, dig, and chisel stone. Again like Ricci, he too came to learn as well as teach, and was ready to discuss with respect the views of others.[30]

Following the directives laid down by St.

Ignatius, Paez concentrated on the court, the nobles and persons of influence. It was the same policy that Ricci had pursued with striking success in Peking. By these tactics, Paez won the admiration of the Emperor, who had long admitted to the superiority of Roman teaching.

In direct contrast to Paez, Mendez' preposterous personality and cast of mind was sickening. He planned to force Roman Catholicism on all the provinces. It was unfortunate for him that his arrival in Ethiopia coincided with a very severe plague of locusts. This was at once interpreted as a visitation of God on the people for abandoning their ancient faith.[31] Their priests and monks had told the people that a cloud of locusts, a sign that they were accursed by God, wherever, they went, followed the Jesuits.[32] Mendez, was unable to recognize that the Ethiopians, *"received the Sacraments more frequently than the customs in the West, fasted more severely, and behaved with greater decorum in the church."*[33]

To summarize, the Portuguese enterprise in Ethiopia began with Da Gama's chivalrous campaign, which briefly saved the country from Islam. Mendez' and Ovidous' approaches were offensive to Ethiopians and the Jesuits intolerance of local traditions and practices were repulsive as we learned above. Paez's mild, broadminded, diplomatic methods came close to success, but only to have his hard won achievements overthrown by the blundering arrogance of Mendez.

The stereotyping of Ethiopian culture and literature has persisted well into the twentieth century. Consider the following statements by Donald Levine,

> The written literature of Ethiopia provides as little scope for individuality as does it's painting. The nature of this literature is to extol sacred objects, not to express individual personality. The *Investigations* of Zara Yacob, a very personal and imaginative critique of prevailing orthodoxies dated in the seventeenth century and reminiscent of the French Philosopher, is the exception that proves the rule; for this manuscript has proved to be a forgery, the work of a Franciscan missionary to Ethiopia in the nineteenth century [...] The effect of this literature has been, as David Riesman suggests is true of written word generally, an individualizing one. It did not serve to "help" liberate the reader from his group and its emotions, and allow the contemplation of alternative responses and the trying of new emotions. Ethiopian religious literature does not invite introspection; it is a corpus to be venerated and solemnly rehearsed.[34]

To say the least this hostile and ignorant statement exemplifies the historical hostility of westerners to Ethiopian history. The jealousies against Ethiopian independence, the grandeur of its history, its resistance to colonial and imperialistic penetration is well known. The brilliant Bernal, in *Black Athena,* has recently documented the roots of this aggression.

Zara Yacob was born to this tumultuous time, a time that was not cognitively capable of tolerating differences. This was an aggressive period that sought to impose one dominant view of Christianity, only one way of being a Christian. This intolerant milieu had a profound impact on Zara Yacob's philosophy as will be shown in the chapters below.

Chapter III
ZARA YACOB: PHILOSOPHER
OF THE HEART

Zara Yacob and Descartes on God

The respected philosopher, Claude Sumner[35], who devoted a lifetime of study to Zara Yacob, has correctly noted that Zara Yacob and Descartes, two eminent founders of modern philosophy, share remarkable similarities. I would like to add, however, that they also depart profoundly on many matters concerning the place of God in human life and the nature of the person. Before I tackle their differences, I would like to briefly summarize their similarities.

Zara Yacob and Descartes were profound religious thinkers. They were such ardent believers that they struggled to make their belief in God a rational faith. For both, God was a rational subject of faith, and that faith itself, they thought, is not beyond reason, but rather is an anchor of rationality. Consider first what Zara Yacob wrote, *"The soul is endowed with an intelligence that is aware that there is a God who knows all, conserves all, rules all... God great and sublime... the reward for our souls, merciful, kind... God created us intelligent so that we can meditate on his greatness."* [36]

Similarly, Descartes wrote in *The Third Meditation*: *"Thus there remains only the idea of God, I must consider whether there is anything in this idea that could have not originated from me. I understand by the name of God a certain substance that is infinite, independent, supremely intelligent and supremely powerful, and that created me along with everything that exists–if anything else exists."* [37]

After profound meditations, they both concluded that God created them, and that there is a creator. Their methods of arriving at that conclusion, however, are profoundly different, as I shall demonstrate below. Beyond these fundamental similarities, many differences arise. Their central differences focus on (1) *Methods of knowing God*, (2) *The meaning of faith* (3) *Conceptions of human possibilities.*

Zara Yacob on Methods of Thinking

For Zara Yacob, the way of thought was prayer. God as the subject and object of thought could only be disclosed to human beings during intense moments of prayer and he believed that prayer itself is guided by intelligence, a faculty that the creator endowed us with. The prayer does not blindly focus on something beyond human reach, the object of the prayer is reachable, but cannot be seen or touched. God is not the object or subject of sensory knowledge. God is the object and subject of thought. God as the symbol of thought,

Zara Yacob believed, could be disclosed to the person in deep prayer, since prayer is the path of thought. One prays to a power outside of oneself, firmly convinced that the prayer will be answered. Strictly speaking the person who prays must believe that there is someone to whom one can pray. Philosophically speaking prayer is a modality of philosophy. It is a highly concentrated and disciplined exercise in thinking. One has to learn how to pray by consulting one's own heart. It is not something that one takes too lightly, as most people do. Time and time again, Zara Yacob asks God to teach him how to pray to him, how to reach and look for him.

Praying to God, however, is a complicated activity. Sometimes, one does not know who to pray to. Different religions have different images of God. The God of Muslims is a different one from the Christian God. The God of the Catholics is different from the God of the Protestants. Even the God of the Ethiopians is different from the European God, as Zara Yacob learned bitterly. These two religions continue to fight vicious wars over the meaning of this God. Many religions continue to stick to a singular appropriation of imagining God, but the idea of God is not subject to a single interpretation, God is the subject of multiple interpretations. These conflicting faiths are anchored upon the dogmatic understanding of God. Talking of this experience, Zara Yacob writes how each faith responds: *"My faith is right,"* they say, *"yours is false. We on the other hand tell them: ' It is not so; your faith is wrong, ours is right... Once I asked a Frang (white) scholar many things con-*

cerning our faith; he interpreted them all according to his own faith…If I had asked the Mohammedans and the Jews, they also would have interpreted all things according to their own faith, then where could I obtain a judge that tells the truth.'"[38]

It is precisely the absence of a judge that led Zara Yacob to engage in *Hassasa* (searching, looking for). Accommodating this daunting task required of him to develop a method of thinking, a method of disclosing God to speak to those who are desperately looking for him. When we agonize over what we should do; how; where, with whom and when, we despair about action and choice, we always hope in vain that God would reveal his wisdom to us. During those great ethical moments, we sometimes hope that a superior intelligence disclose itself to us. As he put it once, *"Oh my Lord and my creator, who endowed me with reason, make me intelligent, reveal to me your hidden wisdom… render me intelligent that I may know your precepts…"*[39] A prayer focused on God is a thought exercise in *Hassasa*, hoping to make the absent God present to consciousness, and a *Hatata*, a relentless form of inquiry, determined to have God speak to the meditating person. Prayer is guided by discovery and uncovering. It is precisely God whom the prayer discovers and whose wisdom the supplicant tries to uncover, so that God's hidden intellectual wisdom and practical guides can inform his/her actions.

The question that haunted Descartes; *"Does God exist?"* is immediately answered; *" I understand there is a creator, greater than all creatures;*

since from his overabundant greatness, he created things that are so great. He is intelligent who understands all...[40]

Once we are so lovingly created, God then expects us to look for him, to be guided by him. This loving God, however, does not want us to live under his tutelage. We are expected to understand him and then use this understanding to be the masters of our destiny, the controllers of our choices. We are fully responsible for our actions, the good and the bad. God has nothing to do with our choices. He certainly does not collaborate with the evil choices we make. Evil choices can be avoided if we think carefully before we act. Prayer can help in this regard.[41] When we pray from the depth of our hearts, Zara Yacob teaches, God responds by empowering us with the practical answer to our agonies and anguish. The prayer focuses our thought on the fountain of practical knowledge, God. That is why prayer was so important for Yacob. For him, prayer is the deepest modality of philosophizing. Prayer gives the human soul a rare joy that cannot be obtained from calculative thinking. Through prayer the lonely self is raised to the summit of Thought, the dwelling place of God.[42]

God dwells inside our hearts. He invites us unconditionally to visit him there through our daily prayer, our meditation. We must submit to his authority, so that he may sense our humility, our finitude. God supplements our inherent finitude with his absolute knowledge, his infinite power, by helping us to overcome our despair, by providing our soul with hope. He gives us hope when we are hopeless. Prayer nourishes our soul with thought. Thought in turn shows us how to habitually nourish our fragile body.

. Zara Yacob's daily prayers are models of philosophical excellence, which I wish to share with my readers in full. An example:

> *You bless my thoughts, my work and my life; give me goods and happiness in the measure that you know and will. Change the heart of men who live with me that they behave well with me; for everything is fulfilled by your blessed will; in my old age stay close to me with your goodness. My lord and my creator, give me joy and felicity, and keep me happy as long as I am on earth; after my death draws me to you and satisfy me fully.*"[43]

Descartes on Thinking

In a striking contrast to Zara Yacob and with a characteristically analytical move, Descartes doubts the fundamental pillar of Zara Yacob's anchor of existence. He doubts, for methodological reasons (so he tells us) the existence of God. Before he believes he wants to be convinced through intellection that God exists indisputably. He begins by doubting his own existence, and by implication, the existence of the being that must have created him. He doubts all the objects that can be directly perceived by the senses. He no longer believes that his hands, his feet and the warm fireplace that is caressing his cold hands are there for the existing being. If he shuts off the senses nothing will be there. His own body suddenly disappears. *First Meditation.*[44] All that remains is thought.

In the *Second Meditation*, he tells us, *"...thought exists; it alone cannot be separated from me. I am; I exist–this is certain...I am therefore precisely nothing but a thinking thing; that is, a mind, or intellect, or understating, or reason —words of whose meanings I was previously ignorant."* [45]

He rediscovers himself anew, not as a body, but rather as a body that exists as a thinking being. The body is displaced by thought; he discovers through the *Second Meditation* that he is a thinking thing. As a thinking thing, he doubts, affirms, denies, wills, refuses, imagines and senses. He thinks that he now sees light, hears a sound, touches a tactile body and tastes delicious food. None of these experiences are real in the ordinary sense. They are real only to the thinking thing. The body that does all this is itself a product of thought. It is the mind that perceives this body that sees, hears, touches, senses and imagines through its various parts, the eyes, the ears and the hands. The body is not real. It does not have an objective reality. Something else has this objective reality.

In the *Third Meditation*, we know that it is only God that has objective reality. If we were to shut off all our senses, there is one power that cannot be stopped. The idea of God remains. Descartes tells us, *"I understand by the name 'God' a certain substance that is infinite, independent, su-*

premely intelligent, and supremely powerful, and that created me along with everything that exists-if anything else exists. [46] God is an infinite substance, whereas man is a thinking being is the central conclusion of the *third meditation.* In the *Fourth and Fifth meditations,* now that he has definitely proven to himself that God exists, he thanks God for giving him a mind and then he states a new rule that says, *"I should never judge anything that I do not clearly and distinctly understand."* [47]

The *sixth meditation* proves that the body is part of the soul, and that the body exists only because it is linked to the mind. So whatever is felt in the body is then simultaneously felt in the mind. A pain for example is registered in the mind before the body feels it. Or, conversely, the body feels it as pain; say in an amputated foot, only because, it is being felt by the mind and this is communicated to the body through the nervous system, because the body itself is part of the mind.[48] To insist that the pain is occurring in the foot, that is no longer there indivisibly, is to succumb to sense deception again. As Descartes put it, *"the pain will be felt as if it were in the foot, and the senses will naturally be deceived."* [49]

I hope that the methodological differences between Zara Yacob and Descartes at grounding their beliefs in the existence of God are clear to the reader. Whereas Zara Yacob began with the unshakable conviction that God exists, and he could search him (Hassasa) and meditate in prayer so that he could disclose himself to the prayer (Hatata); Descartes chose to use his natural reason to prove God's existence. Their differences are crystallized in their methods of investigation. Their conclusions are the same. They are both rational believers.

Zara Yacob on the Meaning of Faith

For Zara Yacob, faith in God is a fundamental human obligation. Faith is something that we choose. We are not born with the capacity called faith. Rather, if we so choose, we can develop the capacity to exercise being faithful to God. Being faithful, however, is the most difficult habit to nurture, considering the nature of our human world, and how miserable life can be. During periods of sustained and painful experiences, it is far easier to be tempted by and to succumb to doubt than it is to fight it and to affirm ones commitment to faith, in spite of the situation, in spite of the pressure of despair and anguish. Drawing from his own experiences with life, Zara Yacob teaches us, *"We cannot, however, reach truth through the doctrine of men, for all men are liars... God sustains the world by his order which he himself has established and which men cannot destroy, because the order of God is stronger than the order of men."*[50] Our choices, Zara Yacob asserts, must then be guided by faith in this powerful God; otherwise we are going to err repeatedly.

Descartes on Faith

In direct contrast to Zara Yacob, faith does not occupy a major space in Descartes' mind. Of course, he writes as a settled believer, but he does not mention faith much. He says very few things about it. Descartes has faith in the idea of God, an idea that he discovered after a systematic doubt. God then is not a given. He once was a possibility, who later became an objective reality, more real than the objects of sense, such as the parts of our body. Once God is proven to be an objective reality, then he becomes an object of rational faith. One believes in this God because one is rationally convinced that he exists. Unlike Zara Yacob, who never doubted the existence of God as an object of faith, a fact that requires no proof, through the use of human reason, Descartes, demands a proof before having faith. Faith is a consequence of rational proof; it does not precede it. Faith follows reasoning. Reasoning is not grounded on Faith, as it is for Zara Yacob.[51]

Zara Yacob on conceptions of Human Possibilities
For Zara Yacob, as I argued above, the possibilities of humans is a corner stone of his Social philosophy and metaphysical descriptions of the self. He is profoundly concerned about human beings and their self-imposed tasks in the care of the self. He repeatedly reminds us that if humans are left on their own, their finitude stands in their way, limiting their actions, restraining their visions, a facticity of the human condition which can be surmounted only if they surrender to God's infinite powers, to show them the way, to put them on the correct moral path. Human laws are necessarily limited; God's laws on the other hand are complete, independent of the influence of the deceptive senses, infinitely powerful, perfect. That is

what human beings hope and can become. They must be informed and completed by God's doctrines[52]

Descartes on Conceptions of Human Possibilities

Descartes' concerns with human possibilities are sparse. They are strictly epistemological and divorced from humans' moral capacities. Not even once does he address morality in his methodological works. It is only through indirect statements that one could hypothesize about our moral life. His epistemological definitions of personhood on the other hand are powerful. He tells us, *"I am therefore precisely nothing but a thinking thing; that is, a mind, or intellect, or understanding, or reason..."* [53] Man in contrast to God is dependent, saturated with misleading senses, unreliable imagination, finite, helpless, subject to errors, created by a supremely intelligent and supremely powerful God.[54]

Modern philosophy, in the sense of personal rationalistic critical investigation, began in Ethiopia with Zara Yacob at the same time as in England and in France (Claude Sumner, *Classical Ethiopian Philosophy*, P. 227.)

And when one comes to Zara Yacob; we are in his debt especially for introducing us to what seems to me to be an extraordinary and original mind grappling with fascinating questions. (Anthony Appiah in preface to *Classical Ethiopian Philosophy)*

Zara Yacob's Treatise

The treatise of Zara Yacob is small but a compete philosophical work addressing itself to all the facets of modern philosophy: metaphysics, morality, and the nature of knowledge. In less than fifty pages, Zara Yacob manages to give us one sustained meditation on life, based on his own long and healthy life

The Story of His Life

He introduces himself movingly,

> *I was born in the land of the priests of Aksum. But I am the son of a poor farmer in the district of Aksum; the day of my birth is 25th of Nahasye 1592, A. D the third year of the reign of King Yakoub. By Christian baptism I was named Zara Yacob, but people called me Warqye. (Golden) When I grew up, my father sent me to school in view of my instruction. And after I had read the Psalms of David my teacher said to my father; This young son of yours is clever and has the patience to learn; if you send him to higher school, he will be master and a doctor." After hearing this, my father sent me to study Zeyma (songs). But, my voice was coarse and my throat was grating; so my schoolmaster used to laugh at me and to tease me. I stayed there for three months, until overcame my sadness and went too another master who taught Qanye (sayings with double meaning) and Sawsaw. (Grammar) God gave me the*

talent to learn faster than my compan-
ions and thus compensated for my previ-
ous disappointment: I stayed there four
years. During those years God as it were
snatched me from the claws of death: for
as I was playing with my friends I fell
into a ravine, and I do not know how I
was saved except by a miracle form God,
After I was saved I measured the depth of
the ravine with a long rope and found it
to be twenty-five and fathoms and one
palm deep. Thanking God for saving me,
I went to the house of my master. After
this I left for another school to study the
interpretation of the Holy Scriptures. I
remained ten years in this type of study; I
learned the interpretations of both of the
Frang and of our own scholars.
Oftentimes their interpretations did not
agree with my reason; but I withheld my
opinion and hid in my heart all the
thoughts of my mind. Having returned
to my native Aksum, I taught for four
years. But this period was not peaceful;
for in the XIX year of king Susaynos,
while Afons a Frang was Abuna, two
years [after his arrival] a great persecu-
tion spread over all Ethiopia. The king
accepted the faith of the Frang, and from
that time on persecuted all those who did
not accept it.[55]

Zara Yacob lived for ninety-three years, without
any reported sickness.

On Knowledge

God is the source of Knowledge. There is nothing that God does not know. Everything that humans wish to know is in the storehouse of God. He is the beginning and the end of knowledge. People must worship this God with all their heart if they wish to partake of this knowledge, or else their wisdom will be incomplete and unreliable. They are advised to engage in *Hassasa*. (Looking for, searching) for this God, when they want to act knowledgably.

God reveals himself to those who genuinely look for him. God is the subject and object of *Hatata* (inquiry, meditation). God himself, who created us in his own image, would like us to partake of his knowledge, without which we are fated to make fatal mistakes. We can avoid these mistakes with the guidance of God. As Zara Yacob put it, "*The creator himself wills that we adorn our life with Science and work; for such an end did he give us reason and power* "[56] Furthermore, "*we ought to know that God does not create us perfect but creates us with such a reason as to know that we are to strive for perfection as long as we live in this world, and to be worthy for the reward that our creator has prepared for us in his wisdom*"[57] God deliberately created us with imperfections, so that we can take life in this world as a challenge, that necessarily requires of us constant improvement, by putting ourselves on the road of moral progress. The development of character becomes a project, and not a finished datum for psychologists to ponder. Reward, God reasoned, would be given to those who strive to be the best, to those who transform potentiality to actuality.

Knowledge for Zara Yacob is obtained through daily prayer. Prayer is a form of philosophizing, a method of thinking, and a vehicle of meditation. It is all three at the same time. Zara Yacob prayed daily, fully convinced that God was listening to his prayer and answering him. The prayer however, needs to be infused with love and grounded on faith and patience. He admits to his readers that when he was young he did not believe in God, and committed many irrational sins. A particular event in his life changes him into a believer, however.

> ...Because of my sins I fell into a trap from which man cannot free himself. I began to be despondent and the terror of death over came me. At that time I turned to God and I began to pray to him that he free me, for he knows all the ways of salvation. I said to God.' I repudiate my sin and I search for your will. But for now forgive my sin and free me[58]

God heard him, so he says, and saved him. This event puts him on a new religious path. From that time on he lives the life of a deep believer. The psalms of David becomes his companion inside that cave to which he escaped for two years, during which time he occupied himself with the content of his philosophical treatise.

He prayed three times a day. His morning and evening prayers were as follows. "O my creator and *guardian! I worship you and I love you with all my heart, and I praise you for the kindness you have shown me this night. In the evening I would say this day, "protect me for the coming day"* [59] He would beg God to help him to use his skills to procure the necessities of life, to bless his thoughts, his work and his life, and to enable him to control his desires through moderation. In a beautiful passage that conveys the power and eloquence of the philosopher's words, he writes,

> *I was admiring the beauty of God's creatures according to their orders, the domestic animals and the wild beasts. They are drawn by the nature of their creation towards the preservation of their life and the propagation of their species. Moreover, trees in the fields and plants which are created with great wisdom grow, bloom, flourish, produce the fruit of their respective seed according to their orders and without error; they seem to be animated. Mountains, valleys, rivers, springs, all your works praise your name...Great are the works of your hands! Behold the sun, source of light and source of the light of the world, and the moon and the stars which you made and which do not deviate from the paths you prescribed for them; who can know the number, the distance and the size of the stars which, because of their remoteness, appear so small; clouds give out showers of rain to make plants green. All things are great and admirable, and all are created with great wisdom.* [60]

He informs us that he remained in the cave for two years marveling at God's greatness and rejoicing God's kindness of protecting him from his enemies. He intensified his prayers, and said, *"I am little and poor in your sight, oh lord; make me understand what I should know about you, that I may admire your greatness and praise you every day with a new phrase."* [61]

Faith

Faith, for Zara Yacob is a personal relationship between the believer and God. Faith looses its power and meaning if it is mediated by third persons, including those self-appointed messengers who claim to read God's mind. Moreover, we misunderstand the nature of faith if we think that it is an irrational belief system that we must blindly obey. Faith is a rational activity that must be cognitively understood. In this Zara Yacob agrees with Descartes, his soul mate, who also argued that Faith is an activity of intellection. Put modestly, faith is a rational activity, although most believers tend to think that faith is inherently blind servitude to God. Even God, the prime mover did not intend those who worship him to do so blindly. For as Zara Yacob reminds us, *"God gave us intelligence so that we can use it to look for him and to meditate about his greatness."*

Zara Yacob asked, *"Is everything that is written in the Holy Scriptures true?"* [62] To answer the question, Zara Yacob confronted the learned scholars of his time and solicited their responses. The results were disappointing in that none of them spoke the truth but only what *"is in their hearts"*, which is to say that they claimed that only their subjective faith was right, whereas all other faiths were wrong. They would glorify their faith and demonize others. This practice infuriated the philosopher. As he put it, " *These days the Frang tell us: our faith is right, yours is false, we on the other hand will tell them, " it is not so; your faith is wrong, ours is right. If we ask the Mohammedans and the Jews, they will claim the same thing, and who would be judge for such kind of arguments?* [63]

These conflicting answers caused the philosopher to wonder about the philosophical status of faith as a vehicle of knowledge. If everyone thinks and believes that only his/her faith is true, and that there is no independent yardstick by which we can measure the veracity of truth, then what is truth, and specifically, what is the relationship between truth and faith? To answer this vexing question, Zara Yacob, prays to God to disclose the answer. He waited silently and patiently. Thinking through the question further, he could only come up with another question, "Why do men lie over problems of such importance, even to the point of destroying themselves? And they seemed to do so because although they pretend to know all, they know nothing. Convinced they know all, they do not attempt to investigate the truth." [64] Referring to David's *Psalms,* he describes such men as having hearts curdled like milk. Their hearts are curdled he tells us because they blindly assume as truth that which they hear from their predecessors instead of investigating truth, which is their birthright. Zara Yacob prays to God to save him from this foundational weakness of the mind. He begs God to make him understand as a rational believer, as a thinking being.

Tormented by the question, he asks again, *"Why is it that all men do not adhere to truth, instead of believing in falsehood"* He answers, *" The cause seemed to be the nature of man which is weak and sluggish. Man aspires to know truth and the hidden things of nature, but this endeavor is difficult and can only be attained with great labor and patience, as Solomon said...Hence people hastily accept what they have heard from their fathers and shy away from critical examination. But God created man to be a master of his own actions, so that he will be what he wills to be, good or bad."*[65]

It is man who determines his destiny by using the appropriate tools furnished by God. The fundamental injunction that humans must follow is that they must use their reason and their intelligence in distinguishing truth from falsehood, genuine persons from liars, good from evil. Reason is there to undertake this irksome but important task. Humans are challenged to rise to this summit of freedom, the site of enlightenment. Intelligence, for Zara Yacob is centered in the heart. The heart as opposed to the brain is expected to enable us to choose correctly. The relocation of intelligence in the human heart is a measured redefinition of reason according to Zara Yacob. Intellection itself is an activity of the heart.

Zara Yacob argues, *"To the person who seeks it, truth is immediately revealed. Indeed he who investigates with pure intelligence set by the creator in the heart of each man and scrutinizes the order and laws of creation will discover the truth."*[66] Truth is revealed not to everybody, but only to those who devote themselves to it. The construction and discovery of truth is preceded by a long waiting period. Truth is an experience of patient waiting. (The quote says the truth is immediately revealed but you say there is a long waiting period) While waiting, one is expected to meditate the greatness of God, the fountain of truth and love. The thinker in despair engages in *Hassasa* and *Hatata* while waiting.

Although understandably tempting, individuals are sternly advised against reliance on the great prophets such as Mohammed, or great leaders, like Moses. They too are prone to make errors in their attempts at interpreting God's holy messages. Moses has made some great errors that should be shunned. It is plainly wrong that Moses considered the act of mating evil, whereas Zara Yacob argues that:

> *Our intelligence teaches us that he who says such a thing is wrong and makes the creator a liar...that marriage springs from the law of the creator: and yet monastic law renders this wisdom of the creator ineffectual, since it prevents the generation of children and extinguishes mankind. The law of Christians which propounds the superiority of monastic life over marriage is false and cannot come from God"*

Nor is Mohammed's teaching that a man could marry more than one woman a law that originated in God.

This is a patently false law with unethical implications. As he put it,

> *"for the law of creation orders one man to marry one woman. If one man marries ten women, then nine will be without wives. This violates the order of creation and the laws of nature and it ruins the usefulness of marriage"* according to Zara Yacob.[67]

Luckily though, *"God has illuminated the heart of man with understanding by which he can see the good and evil, recognize the licit and illicit, distinguish truth from error, and by your light we see the light, oh Lord! If we use this light of our heart properly, it cannot deceive us."* [68] God will reveal his Truth to us. We in turn must heed God's call and listen to the inner light of reason and choose the correct moral paths of reason. The law of reason, as opposed to human laws would teach us that marriage is holy, that it is correct to bury our dead brothers, that we should never abandon our wives lest we force them to adultery, that fasting is unhealthy. The Jews and the Moslems would be wrong to preach otherwise.[69]

However, humans have the capacity to recognize false faiths such as the ones mentioned above. All men are equal, he reminds us; all men are created with intelligence that they ought to use in service of reason. All of us are assigned to love, hope, faith, mercy, and life. God does not discriminate. He does not condemn some to suffering, poverty and death, and others to life, comfort, and joy. He writes, *"But Moses went to teach only the Jews, and David himself said, "He never does this for other nations, he never reveals his rulings to them."*[70] Zara Yacob is angered by this selective assignments of privilege. He is convinced that these deeply flawed human arguments could not possibly emanate from God and that false faith on such ideas must be combated by reason. Zara Yacob was a firm believer that God's reason is manifest in God's doctrines and God's doctrines do not mislead human beings – a point that Descartes also notes, and that I will pursue later.

Yacob also asked himself, *"Why does God permit liars to mislead His people?"* He answered: *"God has indeed given reason to all and everyone so that they may know truth and falsehood, and the power to choose between the two as they will"*[71] Humans can then use reason to defend themselves from liars. But they cannot do this alone. Their human reason must be guided by God's reason, and that they must believe in God's doctrine. We must never rely on human reason, because all men are liars. It is true, that sometimes this world is so cruel, that we are tempted not to believe in God. But that is not the way of reason. There is a purpose for everything and God has his own reasons for subjecting some to suffering, and others to comfort and joy. Those who suffer in the world of appearance will be rewarded later. The human soul does not die. It reemerges later. That is when the body that has suffered in this world will enjoy eternal peace. Zara Yacob believes that, *"this inclination of our nature shows us that we are created not only for this life, but also for the coming world; there the souls which have fulfilled the laws of the creator will be perpetually satisfied and will not look for other things.*"[72] He laments that in this world there is no justice. It is a topsy-turvy world, in which the wicked are wealthy, the righteous are poor, some good men are sad, some bad men are happy. It is only after death that this deformed world will be straightened. Those who suffered in this world will rejoice in the next.[73]

Human Nature

Zara Yacob's conception of human beings is based on his life experiences but always informed by religious vision as inscribed in the Gospels and the bible. He tells us that while he was a teacher, his friends were very jealous of him, because he surpassed them in knowledge and love of neighbor. His independence and critical mind gained him a lot of enemies among Ethiopians and Europeans.

For him, men are fundamentally liars and on the whole are arrogant. Their faith is based on lies, which they present as the truth. Instead of investigating truth for themselves, they lazily internalize other people's beliefs, and hold on to them as if they originated them. Their arrogance contributes substantially to their refusal to investigate the whole truth. They prefer to remain ignorant by following other people's truths, convincing themselves what others say is right. Their laziness reinforces this habit, the archenemy of seeking truth, via one's own mind. Their ceaseless desire for commodities also leads them astray. For the sake of amassing wealth and honor, they will worship other human beings, insofar as they are promised things that they so much desire. They would follow and revere wicked, corrupt and cruel leaders who propagate false faiths, for the sake of securing benefits. They would not stop at doing anything so long as it satisfies desire.

Zara Yacob portrays humans as potentially reasonable- but only if they work on that potentiality, otherwise, they are evil and disposed to lying. But more often than not they do not work on this potentiality and are stuck on the level of immediacy. They have no vision of possibility, in spite of the powerful potentiality that could give them a new self.

Humans are also superstitious and prone to myth making. These tendencies are manifest in the fact that *"they believe wholeheartedly in astrology and other's calculations, in the mumbling of secret words, in omens, in the conjuration of devils, and in all kinds of magical arts and in the utterances of soothsayers. They believe in all these because they did not investigate the truth but listened to their predecessors."*[74] This laziness accounts for the repeated errors that humans continue to make. The world suffers from our refusal to work on our souls- to transform ourselves from the despicable human beings we are, and to avoid the lies that are detrimental because we refuse to change. We are unwilling to challenge ourselves and expunge the accumulation of immoral dirt glued to our character. All these could change if we choose to do so. Yet, instead of cleansing ourselves, we specialize in believing that God wishes that we remained so. We justify false beliefs and erroneous omens and signs by arguing that, *"God did those things, and so they make God a witness of falsehood and a party to liars."*[75]

Although all humans are equipped with the power of reasoning for themselves, rarely do they use this power to investigate the nature of truth. They find it much easier to hide behind prejudices and judgments of others to justify their weaknesses. Moral progress, however, does not take place this way. We can grow gradually, if we learn how to criticize ourselves, if we embark on the path of self-correction. But human beings are too proud for this task, too unwilling to be self-critical. That poses a serious problem that no society has solved. Many educators have come and gone. None of them however, have successfully addressed this problem. They tinker with it. Zara Yacob's brilliance lies in truthfully locating this endemic problem in what human nature has become. He offers some solutions that are convincing only to believers. Non-believers will feel unchallenged by his proposals. His proposals are the following:

First, solving any problem must be preceeded by correctly and carefully identifying the problem. Therefore, the need of cleansing ourselves must be based on the recognition that there is something that we must clean. In this instance, our sedimented habit of simply following other peoples thoughts, judgments, and prejudices which we readily find in customs and traditions, without critically thinking about them violates a fundamental component of one's unique humanity, namely, the use of intelligence. All of us were reminded by Zara Yacob that we are equal in the eyes of God, because he has created us with an intelligence, which can enable us to discover truth through *Hattata* and *Hassasa*. The first rule of reason then is to be cognizant of our power and be critically aware of problems that we can solve through the use of that power if we so choose.

Choice is at the heart of thinking. The nature of choice of course is very complex. Correct choice is predicated on careful thinking, and careful thinking is developed through practice, and practice itself is nothing more than habitual doing of right things. All these moves are remarkably similar to Aristotle's arguments in the *Nicomachean Ethics*.[76] Choice like many human practices can be learned. Good choices motivate us to always choose correctly. They provide us with standards that are worthy to serve as models. Bad choices can also serve as examples of what we must absolutely avoid. They teach us indirectly. Choice is influenced by both practices. Can one consciously choose evil? Zara Yacob asked himself the above question. And he answered, *"But God created man to be the master of his own actions, so that he will be what he wills to be, good or bad. If a man chooses to be wicked he can continue in his way until he receives the punishment he deserves for his wickedness. But being carnal, man likes what is of the flesh, whether they are good or bad, he finds ways and means through which he can satisfy his carnal desire. God did not create man to be evil, but to choose what he would like to be, so that he may re-*

ceive his reward if he is good or his condemnation if he is bad."[77]

I would like to extrapolate some more arguments from this brave argument. Most individuals like to say that we do evil things out of ignorance. Had we known better, we would choose otherwise. According to this dominant view, choosing evil is a consequence of not knowing. However Zara Yacob, like Aristotle before him, thinks otherwise. We choose evil not because we do not know, but precisely because we are accustomed to choosing evil. One can become evil by habitually choosing evil things; one could also become good by habitually doing good things. The question is how does one really avoid evil. The Zara Yacobian response is direct and demanding. Do not choose wicked things if you do not want to become wicked. It is such a simple response, that most individuals do not take it seriously. I want to argue, however, that we should take it seriously and rise to the challenge. Sometimes, although this sounds extremely simplistic, all that it takes to be a good person is that one wishes to be good, and that one assumes that human beings are intrinsically good- and proceed from that assumption. Unfortunately, a substantial number of people are not even convinced that humans are good beings. Rather, they convince themselves that humans are evil, and that we must protect ourselves against evil. Precious time is wasted on fighting evil, instead of trying to be good. Doing well, however, in order to do well is a project, and not a datum; whereas doing evil because human beings are evil, is an ideology that some of us choose. Zara Yacob suggested that all ideologies are prone not to foster original thinking, but blind following of those who "know", out of which emerged a powerful characterization of human beings as followers, although the creator has endowed them with an original intelligence, which they can use and become creators of good values. They can say yes to life and create positive values. Those who subjected the Jews to the torture chamber, and those who consciously enslaved and colonized others chose to do so. They chose wickedness to enrich themselves. Some will mistakenly think that these were classic cases of ignorance moving people to choose evil. I disagree. I think instead that these are powerful cases that prove Zara Yacob's thesis that choosing wicked things produces wicked human beings with wicked characters that easily lead them to choose wickedness over and over again. To make matters worse such individuals even misuse certain religious beliefs as justifications of human nature. In some cases as we learn from Zara Yacob, God is used as the theorist of radical evil. This is a deeply mistaken view. As Zara Yacob put the matter, *"Everything that the light of intelligence shows us comes from the source of truth, but what men say comes from the source of lies and our intelligence teaches us that all the creator established is right."*[78] One possible reading of this lucid passage is that something like radical evil is a human construction that may have nothing to do with man's evil nature. It appears that humans first create the category of evil and then subsume human practices under it, and it traps us humans; by choosing evil we can easily become evil. It is much easier to choose this category than it is to choose the category of good. The first is much closer to our immediate nature than is the second. Becoming good is a potentiality that we must develop into actuality, whereas being evil is what we think is a natural disposition, or, so we have been systematically socialized to believe.

This socialization is powerful, and its effects are devastating. Once it becomes second nature, it is simply impossible to change its course. Humans begin to think that they are naturally evil, and yet according to Zara Yacob, being evil is just one possibility of being human. There are many other possibilities that we can choose, if we want to. God is lurking in the back waiting to help us, demanding that we visit him thorough our hearts and our imaginations. He will listen. He will show us the way. All that we need to do is search, meditate and he will answer. To some he will deliver his presence. To others he will simply show the way. To many he will articulate a correct answer. Each human being will be accommodated differently, relative to ones nature. The Creator knows, but we human beings do not know. Arrogance is our natural tendency.

Humans are not born to live without companionship. It seems that they naturally gravitate toward community, much more readily at least, towards living with one person. According to Zara Yacob, marriage seems to be a natural institution for humans. As he put it bluntly, *"it is not good for man to be alone without a wife; for such a life leads to sin*"[79] In powerful words filled with honesty and respect for women, the philosopher writes, "*There was a certain maidservant of my master whose name was Hirut; she was not beautiful, but she was good natured, intelligent and patient. I said to my master Habtu, 'Give me this woman as a wife'.... I do not wish her to be my maidservant, but my wife; husbands and wife are equal in marriage...for they are one flesh and one life.*"[80] Needless to say, his views of women are remarkably positive. He paints an attractive image of marriage, when it works, as it ought. He has a romantic understanding of love and companionship. He mercilessly attacks all those who taught that marriage is not natural. For some religious thinkers the nature of humans is to be celibate; for others it is to have multiple wives. Zara Yacob disagrees with both. Against the first group he argues, "*Therefore those who believe that monastic life is superior to marriage are themselves drawn to marriage because of the might of the creator; those who believe that fasting brings righteousness to their soul, eat when they feel hungry; and those who believe that he who has given up his goods is perfect are drawn to seek them again on account of their usefulness, as many of our mortals have done. Hence a monk who holds the order of marriage as impure will be caught in the snare of fornication and of other carnal sins against nature and of grave sickness.*"[81] Against the Mohammedans he argues, "*But we know that the teaching of Mohammed could not have come from God; those who will be born both male and female are equal in number; if we count men and women living in an area, we find as many women as men; we do not find eight*

68

or ten women for every man; for the law of creation orders one man to marry one woman."[82] The philosopher is convinced that marriage is part of human nature, whereas monastic life and marriage to more than one woman is not. He thinks that his views are consistent with God's laws, whereas that of other Christians and Muslims is not. In the final chapter I will critically evaluate these views but for now I am merely reconstructing the philosophy of Zara Yacob. A final philosophical evaluation will have to wait for later.

Philosophizing through the Human Heart

At the center of Zara Yacob's originality lies the hitherto unrecognized place of the human heart in philosophical activity. No philosopher before or after him (Pascal, the writer, excepted) had attached such a firm significance to the function of the human heart. Philosophers before and after him tend to ignore the role of the human heart in thinking. For Zara Yacob reason itself is placed in the heart, and not in the brain. It is as if the mind itself is located in the heart, and not outside it. It is because of this that I have called Zera Yacob, the philosopher of the heart.

In classical phrases, he tells us, "*To the person who seeks it, truth is immediately revealed. Indeed he who investigates with the pure intelligence set by the creator in the heart of each [emphasis is mine] man and scrutinizes the order and laws of creation will discover the truth.*"[83] It is the creator who placed intelligence or the ability to reason in the human heart. Hegel much later had argued that nothing great is accomplished without passion. This argument is the closest that philosophers came to recognize the role of feeling in thinking. But this is radically different from Zara Yacob's claims. He is arguing that what we call analytical thinking is itself a function of the heart, and that the heart has been incorrectly described as the organ that processes feelings only. Zara Yacob is contending that thinking is an activity of the heart, and that genuine thinking is passionate, and passion as an expression of feeling is an integral part of thought and not separate from thought. Thought itself is passionate; thought is a passion for truth and feeling grounds truth. He emphasizes again, " *God indeed has illuminated the heart of man with understanding by which he can see the good and evil, recognize the licit and illicit, distinguish truth from error.* " [84]The passion for truth takes place inside our hearts, before it is communicated through language. Speaking the truth or searching for it or meditating about it from the very beginning, is sown in the heart. Truth grows there, and then it explodes in the form of the passion of speech. Our intelligence tells us to do the right things. God withdraws from our everyday lives once he implants intelligence in our hearts. He does dwell in our actions. He has given us the power with which to live the appropriate life of reason. This reasonable God is always available for direction only when we consult him through *Hassasa* and *Hattata*, as I have repeatedly emphasized in this study. Zara Yacob's God is a gentle director; he is not an oppressive God who orders. He directs us

70

through examples, not through harsh command-
ments. He does not tell us what to do; he shows
us what we can do if we use our heart's intelligence correctly. The heart is part of the human
body. However, years of scientific scholarship had
treated the human heart as particularly suited to
absorb and process delicate emotional information. The heart had been so stereotyped that we
rarely think of it as a center of reliable and carefully thought out information. When one wants
to belittle another person's thoughts we are known
to say, "your heart is in the right place", meaning
that you are not thinking well, if you were, you
would not think that way.

Zara Yacob reverses this kind of belief. For him
what we call thinking takes place inside the heart.
The intelligently created being thinks in and
through the heart. This point, Zara Yacob's very
own, is repeatedly underscored in the *Treatise*.
Again he states, " *I know that God answers our
prayers in another way, if we pray to him with our
whole hearts, [emphasis mine] with love, with faith,
and patience: during my childhood I was a sinner for
many years, I neither taught of the work of God nor
prayed to him. I prayed for many days with all my
heart; God heard me and saved me completely; I for
my part praised him and wholeheartedly [emphasis
mine] turned toward him.*"[85] The repeated reference to the heart is deliberate. It is a constant re-
minder to the reader that the creator listens to us
only when we appeal to him from the depth of
sincere thought percolating in the heart. The creator senses the depth of our yearning for guid-

ance, feels the intensity of our anguish, and responds to our search for him. These are the activities of the heart.

Zara Yacob writes, *"I prayed the whole night with a grieved heart. But God had made his heart soft, he received me well and mentioned nothing of the things I was afraid of."* [86] Elsewhere he tells us that when he prays to God, his heart is dilated with joy, and it is during those moments impregnated with thought that he raises himself to God, and God listens to him and reveals his infinite wisdom, that the solitary thinker is despairing to get; believes God too thinks through the heart. The profound wisdom of the creator is given to the heart of the created being. The transcendental intelligence reveals himself to those who genuinely seek his advice, his love, his inspiring hope and his undiscriminating language of justice. To those children of modernity who cannot secure happiness, love and justice by their bootstraps, the reflective intelligence, readily awaits to freely dispose of his guidance and love. When we moderns are lost, distressed, bewildered, all these manifestations of our finitude can be supplemented by the infinity, independence and absolute power of the *reflective* presence. Reflective presence is a name that I gave to God in my Book, *Self-Construction and the Formation of Human Values.*

The reflective presence addresses us in the interiors of our hearts. The lonely human heart is always lost; sometimes the bitterness of life hardens it. At other times, our excessive preoccupation with goods, careers, obligations, and endless ambitions clogs the heart. In such situations the heart is not receptive to thought. The heart is too busy responding to disappointment and physical pain. Sometimes rapacious appetites engulf it. Those frequent mishaps are not good occasions for thought. Effective thought occurs when we are not overly occupied with ourselves. It is then that we can have a place for others. The heart must be emptied of unnecessary burden-the burden of materialism and selfishness. It is much easier to think for ourselves, but the far harder task is thinking for others. Genuine thought must embrace the pains and hopelessness of others as if it is our very own. This kind of thought cannot be done by reason alone. Or, if it must be done by reason, it must be reason infused with the reflective presence. Everything that is worth doing must be done from the heart and by the heart. It must be sincere, modest and critically aware of our contingency. Most importantly, it must be humbled by irony. There are occasions that call for absolute seriousness. Even those painful moments can be quietly accommodated by an ironic comportment. If God can laugh, why should human beings not do the same? Too often we cry when we should not, and we laugh when we should actually quietly meditate. What is worse is that we laugh at things, which we should change and we change things that we should perhaps conserve. Most of the time we do not know how and what to choose. During these confounding moments, awaiting decision, reason becomes helpless. The reflective presence, however, is ready to respond, to the yearnings of the heart, provided that **the created thinking prays**. Zara Yacob tells us that he prayed so many times, and his heart-felt prayers were answered. Prayer from the depth of our heart is a property of our rational nature. This insight originated with Zara Yacob. His modernity stretched the meaning of rationality to include a place for prayer as a natural vehicle of philosophizing. I will elaborate on this theme in my concluding chapter. Consider the following prayers and their outcomes. Zara Yacob informs us that he had sinned for many years, and falling into a trap punished him[87], from which no man could possibly save himself. He was terrified. At that desperate moment he prays from his heart. Soon, he was miraculously saved. He attributed the outcome to divine intervention. This tale, which he is fond of remembering, had a profound effect on his religious philosophy. It is the cornerstone of his belief and his modern rationalistic philosophy. At another instance we are informed that, during his lifetime he had incurred the jealousies of many people. There were those who resented his independence and many others who hated his religious philosophy. The Jesuit priests in particular disapproved of his rational methods of reading the bible. Some openly declared that *"This man is your enemy, and the enemy of the Frang [whites]"*[88] Zara Yacob knew that this was going to put him at odds with the Ethiopian King and the Frang, which it eventually did. So one day the king sent his men and asked him for a visit. Zara Yacob was terrorized, and prayed the whole night. The next day he went to see the king. The king welcomed him kindly, and none of what he thought was imminent happened. Instead, God had softened the

74

King's heart, and the King said to him, *"You are a learned man, you love the Frang, because they are learned. After this the king gave [him] five measures of Gold, and sent [him] away peacefully. After leaving [the King], as [he] still was marveling [at his fate he] thanked God who had treated [him] so well."*[89] Another instance reveals the philosopher thanking God, for hearing his prayers. He shares with us the following incident, *"Remembering that man's path is made firm by God, I said ' direct me, O'lord in the way I should go and to the land I should dwell in. I intended to cross [River Abbay] and to stay in the land [known as] Goffam, but God led me to a place I had not thought of. One day I arrived at Anfaaraz and went to a rich person by the name of Habtu. I spent a day with him. The next day I asked him to give me a paper and ink to write a letter to my relatives in Aksum. He asked me: " Are you an expert at writing? I answered: "Yes I am. He then said: " Stay with me for a few days and copy for me the Psalter of David; I will pay you for this. I agreed and heartily thanked God for showing me the way by which I could live from the fruits of my work."* [90] Thus the philosopher secured a life long work as a writer and teacher of Habtu's children. There are many other instances, but the few that I chose adequately represent Zara Yacob's struggles and the way God intervened and surmounted them. There is a moving passage that I am tempted to quote in which the philosopher sings the praises of the reflective presence. *"God makes his light to dawn for the just and his joy [dawn] for upright hearts; he knows and governs all the ways of our heart; he can make us happy when we are in trouble, and when we are happy. For happiness and sorrow do not come to us as it pleases men, but as God grants it to us. And I said: 'my lord and my creator, give me joy and felicity, and keep me happy as long as I am on earth; after my death draw me to you and satisfy me fully'"* [91]

Philosophy had unjustly ignored the role of prayers in refinancing the "essence" of philosophical activity. I think this is a major mistake and the justification for this move is not convincing enough. The conventional argument is that prayers are religious practices that belong to religious studies and theology. To restrict the status of prayers to the religious realm presupposes that one has to be religious to take prayer seriously, or that one would have to be strictly religious to resort to prayers to begin with. According to this view any person who prays must be religious, and that a non-religious person's prayers mean nothing. To make matters worse, in the philosophical community, a philosopher who prays and dares to enunciate that practice as something that the philosopher does in the classroom is blasphemous. An ordinary philosopher who resorts to prayer, as a way of doing philosophy will subject himself to plenty of insult and neglect. That person will be immediately cast out of the discipline of philosophy. The philosophers of science would ridicule their claim to the philosophical. They would demand that the philosopher first undertake the irksome task of demonstrating the epistemological status of the being to whom he is praying, which is a challenge to which Descartes rose, and proved beyond doubt that his God exists, and that should he pray he knows exactly whom he is praying to. Similarly, Immanuel Kant too, had to convince his readers that his God is not an object of proof [responding to Descartes] but a subject of faith. The two giants managed to defend themselves against their detractors. Ordinary philosophers cannot get away so easily. At the height of the reign of logical positivism, unless one is a descendant of Kant, one would be scorned and castigated for daring to claim a philosophical status if he is caught professing that prayer is a modality of philosophizing, a point that I am arguing on behalf of philosophy.

With the rise of Heidegger, and the emergence of phenomenology, one begins to witness change. Even this school would not readily embrace prayer as a way of doing philosophy. The school *prefers* the nebulous term Meditative Thinking, which it sharply distinguishes, from Calculative Thinking, the latter being a substitute for thinking divorced of mystery, and overly preoccupied with the measurable, demonstrable, clear and "scientific". Heidegeer writes, *"I call the comportment which enables us to keep open to the meaning hidden in technology, openness to the mystery."* [92] It is not far-fetched to link Zara Yacob's stress on thought as prayer with Heidegger's insistence that true thinking is a meditation on the mystery of things in spite of the nebulousness of the idea of *"openness to the mystery"* a cleansing of one's soul with measurability and technological intrusion to the mystery of the world. But there is no mention of thanking the reflective intelligence or God. Heidegger is too much of a philosopher to descend to the level of Zara Yacob's God, the one who created the mystical world of stones, stars, the heavens, the mountains and the lakes that mesmerize us with their sheer beauty. Heidegger comes very close to embracing God, and wishing to get near the fountain of truth, when in *Conversation On A Country Path*, he defines thinking as "moving into nearness"[93]. One could construe this to mean nearness toward the meaning giver, the one who really knows, the uncreated essence, as Zara Yacob conceived of God. One could get near him through thought, through intense prayer of the heart. The famous dialogue ends with Heidegger declaring that this movement into nearness, *"which guided us deep into the night, while wondering upon the depth of the height, if this is released, from whence we are called."*[94]

Meditative thinking is to calculative thinking for Heidegger, as prayer is to ordinary thinking for Zara Yacob. The first seeks to get near the region of the transcendent and similarly the second strives toward God in order to think correctly. In both instances thought seeks to address its contingency by moving toward infinity and completion.

Prayer is a rational exercise. It is motivated by the belief that God is the greatest, and the creator of all that is great. A particular passage drives this point home. Zara Yacob writes:

> *I was admiring the beauty of God's creatures according to their orders, the [domestic] animals and the wild beasts. They are drawn by the nature of their*

creation towards the preservation of their life and the propagation of their species. Moreover trees in the fields and plants which are created with great wisdom grow, bloom, flourish, produce the fruit of their respective seed according to their orders and without error; they seem to be animated. Mountains, valleys, rivers, springs, all your works praise your name. Great are the works of your hands! Behold the sun, source of light and source of the light of the world, and the moon and the stars which you made and which do not deviate from the paths you prescribed for them; who can know the number, the distance and the size of the stars which, because of their remoteness, appear so small; clouds give out showers of rain to make plants green. All things are great and admirable, and all are created with great wisdom.[95]

It is the absolute admiration of God, which encouraged Zara Yacob to presuppose that there is an absolutely powerful creator that he must pray to in order to complete his otherwise dependent self. Unlike Hume in his *Natural Religion*, who drew out the idea of God from habit and custom, Zara Yacob draws it from the belief that there must be a perfect uncreated essence that created the perfect order of things. Habitual repetitions of experiences regulated by the order of the world are not as convincing as firm beliefs on something such as the creator of the world. This is the path that the rationalist philosopher chose. He is

Chapter IV
WALDA HEYWAT'S
TRANSFORMATIONS OF ZARA
YACOB'S PHILOSOPHY

From individual Ethics to Social Ethics

As I argued above, Zara Yacob's philosophy is decidedly individualistic. The individual is the focus of possibilities that he/she could create by the use of God given intelligence. His student, Walda Heywat, on the other hand focuses on social Ethics. There is a marked difference between the priorities of the teacher and the student. I would like to argue that Heywat transforms his teacher's ethics from the solitary individual to the fabric of society, thereby seeking to develop a systematic social ethics. He begins his *Second Treatise* by saying that:

> *Similarly I thought of writing what God taught me during my long life and what I examined with the rectitude of my intelligence, that this book would serve as guide in the counseling and the teaching*

of science to our children, as a stimulant for inquiry on the part of the wise for understanding the works of God and for widening our wisdom. I do not write what I have heard from the lips of men or what I have received from the doctrines of men unless it is what I have examined and know to be good; but I shall write the things which appear to me to be true after I have examined and known them in the eyes of God, from whom I asked in constant prayer and supplications that he show me the truth, and reveal to me his secrets and the way he created man as an intelligent being whom he placed among other creatures which live in this world.[96]

This passage is striking in several ways. The first and most obvious feature is the powerful influence of Zara Yacob on Walda Heywat's worldview. Walda Heywat makes it a telling point in informing his readers that as Zara Yacob taught him, he is using "the rectitude of his intelligence" to investigate the nature of values. This is directly related to the fundamental teaching of Zara Yacob. Walda Heywat, then goes much further, when he announces that he will use his intelligence and pass on what he learned to future generations. Zara Yacob does not reach out to others. He leaves it entirely to the individual to determine his destiny. That is why I have labeled his practice individualistic. Walda Heywat's ethics are programmatic and communicative. He seeks to build a systematic reservoir of knowledge through which others can learn. I am now identifying his ethics in contrast to his teacher's, Social Ethics or Communicative Ethics. His task is to translate Zara Yacob's individual ethics in service of humanity, in this historical context, in service of Ethiopian ethical life.

We are told that men and women in the past have greatly erred because they blindly inherit the prejudgments of others by treating them as knowledge. They never question their parent's beliefs before they form their own. They believe that many things are true just because many people say so. The truth, however, is that many things can be false, but never true, because, *"truth is one."*[97] Similarly, do not blindly believe all that is written in books, since books too are written by human beings. You must test what is written in books against your own experience guided by your own intelligence. The test of a given truth is that it must conform to God's revealed truth, and not to human truth, including the self-proclaimed mouthpieces of God's teachings. As Zara Yacob said, "Falsehood does not come from the Lord, God of truth, but from the error and deceit of men"[98] Stop blaming God when errors occur, blame yourself instead. Anticipating an objection to those who could rightly ask, *"Why should I believe in your writings but not of others?"* He answers, *"I write after a long period of inquiry, prayer and purification of my heart before God; I do not write anything which does not agree with our reason, but only what is in the heart of all men"* [99] One could easily object to this argument by saying that that person does too. The ultimate arbiter I think will be God, who will judge what is in the human heart

and what is not. To those who believe that they
are writing truth, Walda Heywat, reminds them
not to forget thanking God, the God who has
revealed his wisdom to them, because of whom
they too are speaking the truth. He argues that
the yardstick of rationality must at all times guide
the genuine thinker, because,

> *Reason teaches me that my soul is cre-*
> *ated rational that it may know its cre-*
> *ator, praise him, thank him at all times,*
> *and serve [him] according to that ser-*
> *vice that the creator destined for it, in-*
> *vestigate and understand his will in all*
> *the things it does, worship him without*
> *deceit as long as it will be in this life and*
> *in this body.*[100]

Announcing his unique and communicative self,
he adds,

> *Moreover, since God did not create me*
> *only for myself, but placed me in the midst*
> *of other created [men] who are equal to*
> *me, I should live with them in love and*
> *cooperation, and I should not hate them*
> *or do any evil to them...*[77]

One does not need any reason to believe in an
original creator. Of course, it is irrational to believe in anything without inquiry. Man is by nature an inquirer, precisely because he was created
with a faculty that impels and enables man to be
an inquirer and searcher. The creator gave us a
rational soul and intelligence with which to look

for him, and solve the riddles of life. To walk in the light of reason is to be "in the light of God." To be in this light, as Plato announced in *The Republic,* is to experience absolute knowledge. No region of human action escapes the radiant illumination under the power of light; every action is guided by wisdom.

Following his teacher, Walda Heywat too thinks genuine thought cannot be obtained without prayer. As he put the matter, *"If there are people who say: 'Prayer is not necessary, for God knows all our needs, after he created us with those needs, he must give us all that is required for them without paying for that purpose, I say to them: Prayer is not meant to make us worthy of receiving God's favor, and to know from whom we receive what is necessary for our life, and to realize that everything is from the Lord our God."*[101] We are so helpless, weak that the creator knows that we cannot do well without his guidance and blessing-that is why we must pray to him, that is why we should never fail to pay our respects through our thanks. Thanking him is a way of acknowledging our contingency, a realization that when great things happen to us it is because he made it so, and when sorrow saturates us, it is only because he knows that he will empower us to withstand our fate patiently, because it will not last long. He will make it go away. Nothing is beyond God; he is the creator of everything that is and everything that is not. He comforts those who genuinely deserve it. He consoles those who would otherwise vanish because they cannot bear the pain of this world. He punishes those who would otherwise hurt and destroy

85

all those lone individuals who cannot react to power and domination by tyrants.

After these powerful metaphysical reflections Walda Heywat goes on to elaborate the content of his highly intricate social ethics, which are articulated in the form of counsel and advice to his fellow countrymen. His first moral proposition is that a genuine believer must love his neighbors as a matter of duty. Man was not created to be aloof toward others but rather is expected to love others, however, difficult that may be. All human beings ought to help one another. We are instructed not to hate others because of their faith but we must genuinely respect each other's faiths. The customs of a country should be respected. For him customs should not be contested. As a traditionalist the conservation of customs is of grave importance to him. In this he departs from the teachings of Zara Yacob, who was critical of customs and the faiths of others if they were not deemed to be rational. Walda Heywat was an accomodationist, whereas Zara Yacob was a radical critic of traditions. Parents should not be the objects of scorn, however, wrong their views might be. For the time will come when the young will grow old and demand love and respect, so do not do to others what you will not do to yourself. Do not ever let your parents curse you in their hearts.[102] He tells us a wonderful story with a moral import:

> There was an old blind man; one day he
> quarreled with his son; his son was cruel.
> While they were quarrelling, this son, full
> of anger, held his father's leg and pulled

*it over stones and thorns; his father was
weeping and crying in a weak voice.
Whey they reached a well-known place,
the old man cried out and said to his son:
"Let go of me and listen to what I say"
[the son] relaxed his grip and said:
"Speak!" The old man crying bitterly
said the following: "During my youth I
quarreled with my father just as you did
with me today; in my anger I hit him
and dragged him to this place. God the
avenger gives me back today the evil I
deserved* [103]

Education is the pivot to the transformation of
the self. Following his teacher's path, Walda
Heywat argues that true education ought to be
multidimensional. The investigation of truth must
take into account the imperativeness of knowing
many doctrines, so as to choose the one doctrine
that is the most rational. Like, *"the bee which col-
lects honey from the flavor of the field: it does not stop
at one flower or at one field, but it goes from one to
another, gathers from all and produces two elements
[...] if you gather wisdom from all doctrines you can
obtain two elements: the honey of good deeds which is
sweet and uplifts your heart, the ways of your doctrine which spring for the light of your intelligence,
that it will serve as lamp for the blind of the earth
and the illiterate and will expel darkness from the
heart of those who sleep in the night of ignorance and
are in the darkness of their foolishness."* [104]

Thought is sharpened by the frequent use of
the mind, and the body is maintained through repeated use of the appropriate body part, such as

the hands, which are created to do handicraft. There is no substitute to working with one's hands, we are told. For Walda Heywat, working with one's hand is God's precept, since God himself created this world with his own hands. Laziness is an abomination. Every human being should live by the fruits of one's own labor. He writes, *"Acquire as much as you can without dishonesty; enjoy all the goods you have acquired by the sweat of your brow, and be like the creator: as our creator created from nothing by his power and wisdom all the goods of this world that we see so you also produce by your own effort and wisdom from you work some good fruit for your life and that of your fellow man."* [105] No one should appropriate what he did not create. The person who created it must appropriate value, and the surplus must be shared with the genuinely needy, this is the conclusion one can cautiously draw from the argument. As he put it, *"Do not be harsh towards your fellow man; if your passions are great, give out much: if you have only little, share it with those who are needy and who are poorer than you: he has created together the rich and poor, strong and weak, so that we may help one another and strengthen ourselves with mutual charity."*

Closely following his teacher's philosophy, he too thinks that fasting is unnatural as well as unwise. It unnecessarily jeopardizes one's health. God demands that we eat when we are hungry and drink when we are thirsty. Nowhere does God's precepts command us to fast; God prefers that we thank him for providing us with food and drink. Those who preach otherwise do not understand God's wisdom. [106]

The care of the self is also God's precept. He advises that we wear clean cloth, that we wash our body frequently and live in a spacious house with good lighting. We should cleanse our soul from backbiting, adultery and theft. One of his noble advices is that *"You ought to weigh your words on scales of your wisdom before they come out from your heart; otherwise, once you will have uttered them out of your ignorance, your ̄ʼegret will be useless. Remember that a word is not better than silence, but that silence is better than all words, and that a talkative person cannot live in peace on earth."*[107]

There are three things that we should be wary about. They are the tongue, the hands and the genitals. Misusing any of these bodily parts produces dangerous results. The misuse of our tongue leads to avoidable quarrels and resentments; the uncontrolled use of sexuality yields adultery; and an undisciplined hand rests on other people's property, leading to theft. Some of his most original advices pertain to the right way of living, methods of bringing up children, the role of culture, happiness and hope, prudence, anger and pride, and God's rewards for the right way of living. I will briefly summarize his original contributions in these areas.

The pivot to the right way of living is self-awareness. One must be critical of ones self - one's defects and strengths. Without a critical knowledge of self, a person cannot develop character, because character is built on needs, and needs cannot be decided before knowing what we genuinely need more or less of. All human beings have vices of one kind or another. To deny this fact is to be unaware of self. In a shockingly sexist view, he writes, *"O man, remember that a woman is weak by nature and less intelligent than man. Therefore, bear patiently with the harshness of her nature and the loquacity of her tongue: let her anger pass away, not giving it too great importance, and never quarrel with her."* [108] This disappointing passage is in sharp contrast to his teacher, Zara Yacob, who had a remarkably progressive view of women as the absolute equals of men. Recall the following passage that I quoted earlier, where Zara Yacob had eloquently written, *"husband and wife are equal in marriage; we should not call them master and maidservant; for they are one flesh and one life."* [109]

Marriage is holy he argues, exactly like his teacher. Monasticism is unnatural. He essentially repeats what he has learnt from Zara Yacob. Monasticism destroys the order of the world, as God intended it. He and Zara Yacob are obsessed with this argument. The argument is a reaction to the culture of the seventeenth century that incited dogma calling that monastic life is one of God's fundamental precepts. The two philosophers are out to dismantle this paradigm, which they think is irrational, by replacing it with a rational precept that wants to free desire from suppression. As he put it:

> *Monastic life is man-made, while marriage comes from the law of nature and the will of the creator who instituted it."* [110]

Be considerate to your wife' needs. In an enlightened and modernistic passage, uncharacteristic of
the time, he writes,

> *Draw near your wife marveling at and*
> *praising your creator, and when you sleep*
> *with her do not seek the pleasure of the*
> *conjugal act for you alone, but render it*
> *also pleasant for your wife and do not*
> *deprive her of the portion of pleasure that*
> *God gave her: therefore do not be hasty,*
> *but linger a little until she is also grati-*
> *fied by the act, so that her pleasure will*
> *not remain less than yours or be weak-*
> *ened. If you do not make it a gratifying*
> *act for her, she will suffer pain and de-*
> *spise you, and your marriage will not re-*
> *ceive God's blessing. Do not listen to those*
> *who say that the conjugal act is filthy*
> *and that one in it a destructive odor and*
> *a darkness that has no utility; those who*
> *speak such things deny their creator.*"[111]

Divorce is against God's Law so, if you can, pre-
serve your marriage. He writes,"*The fickleness of*
our nature makes man believe that another woman
would be better for him, and makes a woman believe
that another husband would be better for her. There
is no use in replacing a wife with another wife or
husband with another husband: but it is to your in-
terest that you beautify your first marriage entered
upon by the will of God"[112]

There is an art that we must learn to live well.
The fundamentals of that art is the knowledge of
the self and the recognition that to be human is

to be privy to imperfection. Self-knowledge ought to begin with this awareness. A man must also be aware of gender differences; he must know for example that a woman is weaker and less intelligent than a man. Man therefore should bear *"with the harshness of her nature and the loquacity of her tongue."* Get used to her imperfections, and life will be easy.

The woman should also be aware of her husband's weaknesses. She should delight him with fine food and drink and if she loves him, he cannot hate her. She should impress him with her diligence and patience.

The bringing up of children is a major theme in Walda Heywat's mind. He advises us to be patient with our children, to not lose our temper with them; to keep the perspective that we too were brought up by parents who must have borne a lot. He says we ought to punish them for the right reasons and at the right time and chastise them not for breaking objects, but for other more fundamental reasons, such as: malice in their hearts, stealing, calumny, pride, disobedience, anger, slothfulness, curse, plunder, fornication. Punishing them for these things when they are very young will prevent overlooking these vices, which can result in the loss of virtue, and consequently in the damage of the self. He writes, " You also should fear for your children and bring them up in the fear of God and in the knowledge of what they should do. When you admonish your children, do not admonish them with anger or with words of curse but with words of wisdom and counseling so that they understand the chastisement is for there own benefit and utility. Always teach them and instruct them with words of doctrine, maxims, stories and examples of other men so that they may stop them from doing evil and learn to do well. Teach them how to write, acquaint them with knowledge and books."[113] Ignoring your duties of raising your children properly is a sign of serious irresponsibility. Your children will later blame you for it. Most fundamentally you will have violated God's expectations, for which you will never be forgiven. The cultivation of virtue is not the duty of teachers, as is often assumed, but is the foundational obligation of parents; parents are the primary teachers of their own children.

One of Walda Heywat's teachings is that the wealthy and the powerful are not the models of virtue but the patient and the wise are. Although patience is bitter to exercise, its results once it is carried out are sweeter than sugar and honey. As he put it, "Never forget there is a time for everything that all things that are not done in their proper time bring about misery and a great affliction, that the science of the time for everything is a great wisdom of a greater value than all other doctrines."[114] He tells us that time and cultures are the parents of character; character matures in the vast womb of time. Many great persons have been wasted because they ignored time and culture. Unlike his teacher, who was a radical critic of custom, his student preaches that the prudent person abide by the customs of the country of which one is a citizen. For him all periods have good and bad sides. Strictly speaking, there is no bad period, but rather bad persons. There are good times because there are good persons. There are bad times because there are bad persons. There are bad periods sometimes, because God made it so. We cannot change the course and the moods of time that have been decided by God. These are marked periods that cannot be changed by human will. We have to go through them, until God determines to change the time, if he so decides. Otherwise, our duty is to patiently bear the bad time.

Be selective in your trust of other human beings. Beware that not all humans are worthy of your trust. Considering the nature of humans, which is essentially bad, do not even unconditionally trust your friends. Be particularly careful in dispensing with your secrets to your friend. Once you disclose your secret to a friend, you are bound to your listener. This advice is remarkably similar to Machiavelli's advice to the prince.[115]

He further says that prudence must be enlightened by caution. Also, the prudent life must be free of anger. Similarly, we must also shun pride and vanity and avoid the company of vain and proud people. We must not seek to excel at the expense of others and be even tempered; he believes that we will find peace in this condition, rather than in the competitive life. He writes, *"He who searches for glory and prominence among men will be affected by disgrace, stained by insults; the jealousy and hatred of all men will turn against him."*[116]

He says that the prudent man knows what is due to him and what belongs to God and that seeking authority over the lives of others is ultimately God's domain. Compassion, love, justice, comforting others is the language of prudence. Those who comfort others when they are sad, those who feed them when they are hungry, who cure others when they are sick, who visit the poor, who genuinely share the sorrow of others, will be amply rewarded by God. The creator is never blind to good or indifferent to the bad. The created being might not see God's actions but God is always responding to the human condition.

And, if we must exercise authority over others, we must not oppress them and justice towards all must be the supreme principle of our governance. He reminds us that the creator is always just and we must treat the poor and the rich with the same measure of justice. Our disposition should be compassionate and passionate and we should care for those whom we wish to govern as we would our children. If we oppress them and terrorize them, they will curse us in their hearts, and God will listen to them. God will punish us; he is an ever-vigilant God, who rewards good deeds, and punishes oppressors. Like Machiavelli before him, he too preaches that the ruler must be loved rather than feared.

Hope is given to us because we are so prone to hopelessness. When we fall ill, we become hopeless. Walda Heywat advises us to behave otherwise. He tells us to bear our affliction patiently; to face it courageously; to trust in the mighty creator, who will change our situation and to search for him. He might not respond in our lifetime, but we can be certain that he will reward us when we face him in the other life. We will be liberated from our misery through death. In death:

"*You will enjoy perfect bliss, and possess perpetual and infinite beatitude. Do not love the absurdities of this world–a world in which you must remain until your term of servitude and trial is completed.*"[117]
We must not be afraid of death – Death is liberation. But life – Life could be servitude. Some are chosen to live the good life here. If they do not live it rightly, they will live in eternal servitude later. Others are fated to suffer in this life. If they bear it patiently and courageously, they will live in eternal beatitude in the other life. Our destinies are marked. Every one of us is fated to die. In death we shall encounter our dues face to face with God. His brilliant meditations end with the following song of the heart, "But you my bother, who accept and approve my counseling do not be afraid at the hour of death, for it better for you to go to your creator. Oh! Is not freedom more valuable than servitude, joy than sadness, and life than death? Likewise, it is better for the soul to be liberated from the prison of the body than to be bound to it. As a man freed from prison sees the light of the sun which gives him delight and heat, likewise our soul, come out of the body, will contemplate God's light and will burn with love for its creator; turning back it will glance at the loss of this world and say with astonishment; "How could I love that ignoble servi-

tude? How did I fear a death, which brought me into this beatitude forever and ever? Amen"[118]

Chapter V
ZARA YACOB AND THE
PROBLEMATIC OF
AFRICAN PHILOSOPHY

The question of African philosophy was not even born during Zara Yacob's time. Both Zara Yacób and Walda Haywat were fortunately unburdened by it. Their problematic was a different one. Throughout the *Treatise* we hear Zara Yacob bitterly complaining about the *Frang* as constantly and relentlessly harassing Ethiopian priests to convert to Catholicism, to renounce their primitive ways, to rebaptize by force if necessary. There are shocking statements of rebuke, ridicule, and utter disrespect of Ethiopian customs. The Ethiopian ways of eating, of worship, of seeing, are all indiscriminately condemned. The culture as a whole is described as irrational, hero worshiping, custom bound, anti-modern, and anti-reason.

This was Zara Yacob's universe in the seventeenth century. The ambience was hostile to the flourishing of the individual. One can imagine the suspicious eyes of the Frang who were scrutinizing the movement of this solitary thinker, a rebel,

an original worshipper, grounded in the Ethiopian soil, but unafraid to replace some of the dirty
soil with fresh soil of his disciplined and original
Hassasas and *Hatatas.* This unusual cast of mind
perturbed the Jesuit teachers, who came to convert the "primitive" Christians to their "enlightened" ways. The philosopher refused the conver-
sion in his heart, without betraying his secrets to
anyone. It is through this colonizing gaze that
something similar to the problematic of African
Philosophy began to implant itself in the sover-
eign state of Ethiopia.

The Jesuits were questioning the capacity of
Ethiopians to imagine God in a rational way. What
they sought was to be the source of a correct worship of God, which could then be imposed on
Ethiopians. It is precisely on this foundational
interpretive level that Zara Yacob opposed the Jesuitical interpretation of the idea of God. His resistance was interpretive. His intelligence did not
agree with their ideas of God's doctrines. His was
not a patriotic disagreement. It was purely philosophical. He was convinced that his individual
interpretation was more rational than that of the
Frang. He did by no means use a dominant Ethiopian paradigm to resist a European one. He was
equally resistant to certain irrational and unreasonable Ethiopian practices, which put him at
odds with Ethiopian religious figures, some of
whom turned out to be fierce opponents, who later
reported him to the Ethiopian catholic King. Zara
Yacob's case perfectly fits the image of the lone
philosopher whose passion for truth puts him at
odds with any society.

At issue is the question of God as a project of interpretation by a gifted thinker, an *"extraordinary and original mind"* [119] Paulin Hountondji is right to argue that, *"When I speak of African philosophy I mean that literature, and I try to understand why it has so far made such strenuous efforts to hide behind the screen, all the more opaque for being imaginary, of an implicit 'philosophy' conceived as an unthinking. Spontaneous, a collective system of thought, common to all Africans or at least to all members severally, past, present and future, of such-such-such an African Ethnic group."* [120] His point, which is essentially correct, is that philosophy is a critical practice of an individual thinker. It is not a group orgy. The group is less important as a practitioner of philosophy, and more useful as a source of problems and occasionally as depositories of virtues that could be elevated into philosophies by the activities of an individual thinker. This is precisely what Zara Yacob tried to do in seventeenth century Ethiopia. He immersed himself in the culture and remerged to the surface as a critique, a beacon of Enlightenment. He initially paid a heavy price for this criticality; It cost him exile. But it also produced literature, a written work that I am seeking to engage at the moment. Philosophy in this strict sense is an individual enterprise. It is critical, dangerous, detached, and in perpetual tension with time and culture. It progresses, very much like science, by dismantling the past, by criticizing groupthink and patriotic self-congratulation. It is fueled by the passion for truth. Zara Yacob did not challenge the Frang as an Ethiopian - he challenged them as an original thinker, a critical philosopher, a rational believer, in tension both with his own society and that of the Jesuitical evangelists, who claimed to be the mouthpieces of God.

It is in this sense that he sought to originate a philosophy written by an Ethiopian thinker, against the background of an Ethiopian, African culture. We can now claim with Hountondji that there is an African literature, a philosophy of culture that we must critically read and assess. Zara Yacob writes as a philosopher on the meaning of God, on reason & rationality, on human nature, and on faith & virtues. He engages these perennial themes of philosophy and while doing so he initiates what has been charted in the twentieth century as African Philosophy.

What is the nature of African Philosophy? Numerous philosophers have responded to this question. One of the most exciting of them, Paulin Hountondji, the Beninois philosopher, has written, *"By African Philosophy I mean a set of texts, specifically the set of texts written by Africans and described as philosophical by their authors themselves."*[121] Zara Yacob's treatise is philosophical when measured against this definition. Of course, Zara Yacob would say it is vain and in bad taste to label one's own work as philosophical. It is philosophical however, according to the definition, because the author participated in the articulation of a perennial philosophical problematic, namely, the idea of God and the meaning of faith. The Treatise of Zara Yacob introduces a unique way of doing Africa Philosophy. Zara Yacob attempts to encourage believers in general, and Ethiopian

believers in particular, as I argued above, to liber-
ate themselves from bondage to groups, institutions, religious leaders, in their quest to live their
lives according to God's doctrine. Human doctrine, he powerfully argued, leads to tutelage to
those who claim to know. As we recall he singled
out Mohammed and Moses for the attack. He
does not attack them as a doctrinaire or even as a
particular kind of Christian. He disagrees with
their respective interpretations of God's doctrine.
His lamentations are strictly philosophical.

His work is a contribution to a radical orient-
ing of African Philosophy in another sense. African philosophy must be ground on reason, that
peculiar task of intelligence. Numerous efforts
have been made to identify a peculiar essence of
African Philosophy. Sadly, for Zara Yacob, and
Hountondji, Masolo and Wiredu,[122] there is no
singular essence that we can call African. For Zara
Yacob in particular, as he is the first African to
have boldly done so, reason is the essence of philosophy. By definition, that same reason is the
essence of African philosophy. It is a clear and
uncompromising thesis that humanizes Africans
as cognitive beings like every other human being.
In his bitter disagreements with the Frang, what
is striking is that he does take not them on as a
nationalist proudly resisting hegemonic cultural
penetration. That concern does not bother him
as much as the falsity of the meaning of God that
the Jesuitical interpretive was saddled with. For
him the Jesuitical preachers did not have reasonable interpretations of God's doctrines. They lied.
Their discourse when assessed by pure intelligence

inscribed in the human heart was found to be disturbingly faulty. Zara Yacob's self-imposed mission was to emerge with a reasoned discourse at the service of humanity. Not even once does he identify himself as an Ethiopian resisting colonial discourse. This absence of national consciousness is originally Zara Yacobian. His commitment to truth, his passion for God, transcends the parochialism of nationalistic philosophy. The purity of his heart is most impressive and unusual among national philosophers. The main Jesuitical evangelists, as I argued in chapter 1, were consciously nationalistic. Their commitment to their European heritage was ingrained deeply into their thoughts. The opposite is true of Zara Yacob. His search is the God of reason. He meditates about and prays to this Universal God, convinced that he is going to reveal himself to those who are desperately looking for him, patiently waiting for his disclosure, his appearance to the world. He is waiting, preparing himself for a face-to-face encounter in the company of a quiet and deep prayer.

As is well known, African philosophy has been sometimes essentialized as being anchored in emotion devoid of reason, at other times it has been characterized as an activity of groups denying the individual- any active role to think for herself, at other desperate times, it has been defined as anti-reason. Zara Yacob and Walda Heywat simultaneously freed African Philosophy from these cumbersome and dehumanizing essences. Thanks to both these mighty thinkers the dignity of the African person is restored. Because of their contributions, African individuals are now allowed, should they desire to choose the philosopher's vocation, to unapologetically and confidently choose philosophy as a stylistics of existence, an ethics of good living. Not that philosophy has any special status to claim, it does not, but only that philosophical activity is a transformative possibility that one could choose as a way of life. Thanks to both these thinkers, one need not think as the enemies of the African individual have argued that, to choose the philosophical path is to choose the western path. This deeply flawed and historically inaccurate hegemonic claim by the west has now been shattered. Philosophy is a universal activity exactly like language is. It is a practice that any human being could claim. Its pivotal center, reason, is also a universal faculty that human beings are endowed with, as Zara Yacob so masterfully argued. This particular view of philosophy, needless to say is not beyond rebuke. Indeed Zara Yacob and Walda Heywat do claim many things that their followers have to be willing and able to defend. In the two chapters that follow, I attend to the attacks of reason from the postmodern angle. Embracing this rationalistic view of philosophy, which I have made my own, requires a defense, against certain Afro-centric essentializing of philosophy as anti-reason, which I move to immediately.

Chapter VI
ZARA YACOB'S PLACE IN THE
HISTORY OF PHILOSOPHY

> *There are two great myths about phi-*
> *losophy in Africa. The first is that there*
> *can be subtle reflection on the great meta-*
> *physical and normative questions of hu-*
> *man life only in literate traditions. The*
> *second is that there are in Africa no ex-*
> *tended literate traditions of metaphysi-*
> *cal and normative reflection, save those*
> *in Arabic scripts, whose cultural roots are*
> *in Islam. (Anthony Appiah, Preface to*
> *Classical Ethiopian Philosophy)*

The discovery of Zara Yacob's *Treatise* is a major philosophical event in the history of African philosophy. In this chapter I attempt to accomplish two interrelated tasks. The first is dismantling the two myths by creating a space for Zara Yacob's rationality of the heart in service of humanity. For his vision of reason is a radical corrective to the modality of reason that became paradigmatic in the nineteenth century in Europe, with the diffusion of the enlightenment project. My second purpose, narrower than the first, is to secure Zara Yacob's place in the history of philosophy.

Consider the following two paragraphs below:

> *Enlightenment is man's release from his self-incurred tutelage. Tutelage is man's inability to make use of his understanding without direction from another. Self-incurred is this tutelage when its cause lies not in lack of reason but in lack of resolution and courage to use it without direction from another. 'Have courage to use your own reason' — that is the motto of the enlightenment.*[123]

> *To the person who seeks it, truth is immediately revealed. Indeed he who investigates with the pure intelligence set by the creator in the heart of each man and scrutinizes the order and laws of creation will discover the truth.*[124]

The author of the first, justly famous paragraph is Immanuel Kant and Zara Yacob is the author of the obscurely known second paragraph. Kant wrote the first paragraph in 1785. Zara Yacob wrote his unknown statements almost a hundred years earlier in 1667. The author of the first is the internationally known German, European. Zara Yacob, the author of the second paragraph, is an Ethiopian, an African. Zara Yacob had the *psalms* of David as constant companion and inspiration, but was ignorant of philosophical discourses, outside of his homeland. Kant was not familiar with the works of the Ethiopian thinker who struggled with *The Treatise* from the plateaus of Ethiopia and Zara Yacob was not familiar with the works of one of the world's master philosophers. But, a close reading of the two paragraphs, which are a century apart, gives the reader the impression that they are asserting in two different languages, and against the backdrop of radically different experiences, the same conviction, the same intense passion for truth through the vehicle of reason.

In light of these facts it is shocking that the Enlightenment has been housed in Europe, and philosophically put in Kant's intellectual safe box, to which only Europeans had an access. This trend continues unabated and uncorrected. I would like to make a modest contribution toward correcting that discourse. This historically inaccurate genealogy of reason needs a careful rethinking, for the sake of human beings.

Reason, a distinct faculty, belongs to all of us. It is sacrilegious to make this human faculty an attribute of a particular race. All cultures and their language systems in one way or another do have a limiting condition of human action. Reason is that limiting condition. All cultures do not exonerate everything that humans wish to do. Some actions are tolerated less than others; some values are universally practiced while others are universally condemned or disapproved. Justice, for example, is a cultural universal that is highly idealized. Murder and rape are cultural universals that are widely deplored. Kwasi Wiredu is quite right when he reminds us that, *"Whether you are a Ghanaian or an American or a Chinese or of any other nationality, race or culture, truth telling is an inde-*

fensible obligation. To trifle with such an imperative is, quite plainly, to be immoral in a very strict sense."[125]

Paulin Hountondji is equally convincing when he argues, "If all men are natural metaphysicians, it is by virtue of the very nature of reason which irresistibly impels it to break out of the of the field of experience by following up the series of its conditions as far as the ultimate unconditional. This motion is irrepressible in all men, in all cultures. In this respect, Western civilization enjoys no special privilege: reason is doomed to the same fate everywhere."[126]

These two African philosophers and many sympathetic others are aware of the ways by which Africans have been stereotyped as immoral and unreasonable creatures who have no innate sense of reason, reason understood as the limiting condition of unchecked and unregulated desire. What does it mean for one to be reasonable, and more specifically, for a given philosophy to be anchored on reason?

The reasonable person is one who is acutely aware that as a created being he/she is endowed with a faculty of intelligence that is so powerful that it enables one to think and choose correctly. This created being, however, as a thinking being, is finite and dependent, and therefore must draw the sufficient and necessary power to think and choose correctly by engaging in (*Hassasa* and *Hattata*), from an outside power; That power is God. Reasonableness, then is the knowledge of the human self' limits and contingencies. The capacity of knowing begins with the Socratic hu-

mility that one does not know. The Zara Yacobian
notion goes deeper than Socrates' secular humility, in that, it introduces the non-believer to the
view that complete knowledge is not man's right.
It is a divine power that is revealed to the believer.
If one is to ever know, then one must begin with
faith, faith in God, the substantial house of reason. For Zara Yacob reason has a transcendental
dimension. One is reasonable, as in the scientific
tradition, not because one could reckon, calculate,
detachedly analyze, or replicate experiences, but
fundamentally because one knows that human
tools in and of themselves are not enough unless
they are complemented by a transcendental power.
The idea of God completes the idea of reason. In
some Hegelian quarters, one could assert that
Reason itself is a metaphor for God. Zara Yacob's
claim is couched differently. He does not equate
God with reason. Instead, he argues that God has
given us intelligence with which to think and
choose correctly. Correct thoughts and choices
are ground on reason, or else they will loose their
substantiality and correctness. The solidity of correctness requires the disclosure of God's presence.
The reasonable person seeks to have an access to
God's wisdom through heartfelt prayer. Prayer is
not the practice of irrational, mad and desperate
souls, as some scientists assert. Prayer is a vehicle
for reasoning. It is a practice of reason, a way of
communicating with the wisdom giver. More specifically, prayer is a method of searching truth,
meditating about meaning, the meaning of our
existence.

The fragility of existence and the slippery nature of human life are carefully diagnosed by Zara Yacob, and Kant after him, as needy of a power much stronger than man. Both Zara Yacob and Kant insist that reason without God is blind. It is God that illuminates the darkly lit room of reason as a tool of calculation. The hubris of the reasonable man is corrected by adopting a different way of reasoning. It is Zara Yacob, in the seventeenth century, who provides that original reconstruction of reasonableness. His notion of reason is a humbling one. The tools of modernity: reason, agency, rationality, predictive power, and mathematical precision are shown to be inadequate, unless supplanted by an ordinary form of reason wrapped by God.

Our very own reasoning power is fragile and brittle, when left to its own devices. The creator intended it so. He deliberately creates us in this way. He makes us imperfect, so that we can seek perfection; he makes us incompletely self-determining so that we can look for him-outside of ourselves; he subjects us to uncertainty, anguish, despair, hopeless and helpless, so that we can search him to release us from our suffering; he sculpts us with easily breakable bodies, so that we may seek his guidance in taking care of ourselves; and he constructs us as natural beings unknown to ourselves but with mighty curiosity to study our nature.

And while studying nature, we become hypnotized by the power of technology we develop, that we forget the creator. We begin to play with fire and subject ourselves to be devoured by our own creation. God laughs at us as we make fools of ourselves; we mock him, we deny his existence, we ridicule those who love and believe in him... all the while God continues to laugh at us.

Our rational nature, however, requires that we consult God when we are genuinely thinking. Prayer is the form that our communication with God requires; praying is a daily conversation with God. However, learning how to pray is not an easy task, prayer is a profound and solitary way of reaching God; it requires years of conditioning and discipline. It is very easy to forget praying to God, particularly when we are distracted by other unimportant matters: watching a TV program, talking to a friend on the phone, listening to the radio, or sheer laziness.

We think that we have too much or more important things to do, to be bothered by this God thing. What is easily dismissed as a "God thing" by some people (philosophers included) is a fundamental component of Zara Yacob's constitution and rationalist philosophy. The soul "endowed with intelligence" actively looks for God. It is this transcendent power that knows, feels, desires, guides and teaches us all.

To keep matters in perspective, consider what Aristotle says about reason. Generally speaking, reason *(logos)* is the capacity with which humans formulate rational principles. On this view, the reasonable person is the one who knows how to apply rational principles to the choices that that person makes. This is particularly true of the practically reasonable person. Aristotle writes,

Now happiness is activity in conformity

113

with virtue, it is to be expected that it should conform with the highest virtue, and that is the virtue of the best part of us. Whether this is intelligence or something else which, it is thought, by its very nature rules and guides us and which gives us our notions of what is noble and divine; whether it itself is divine or the most divine thing in us; it is the activity of this part (when operating) in conformity with the excellence or virtue proper to it that will be complete happiness.[127]

He added, *"A man whose activity is guided by intelligence, who cultivates his intelligence and keeps it in the best condition, seems to most beloved by the gods."* [128] The parallels between Aristotle, allegedly a non-believer, and Zara Yacob, a proud believer, are arresting. Both are desperately looking for a power outside of themselves who can give them genuine power-so that they can depend on themselves and attain happiness. The truly happy man, Aristotle emphasizes, *"can study even by himself, and the wiser he is the more he is able to do it"*[129]

In a similar spirit, Zara Yacob writes, *"Alone in my cave, I felt I was living in heaven. Knowing the boundless badness of men, I disliked contact with them […] there I lived peacefully praying with all my heart on the Psalms of David that God was hearing me."*[130] Both these thinkers, through different routes, came to realize the benefits of solitude, the indispensability of dwelling in the interiors of the heart to consult a divine power. Aristotle equivocates between thinking that there may be a divine power outside, as Zara Yacob definitely believes, that there is a divine thing in us that Zara Yacob denies. Zara Yacob goes outside of the self in search of a divine power. Aristotle wonders if we ourselves may not be capable of divinity when we ultimately become wise. At any rate both of them are convinced that true knowing is a divine activity. At the minimum it requires withdrawal from human affairs, from excessive presence in the world. Thought demands silence. The human heart is the most silent place to which thought takes an abbot, discovers an intimate interior. Inside the heart the thinker confronts himself/herself and celebrates life and death-courageously and honestly. There is no hiding in the company of the divine power. The divine knows every human move. Therefore we cannot hide.

No fear. No hesitation; only thought, pure knowing. Hiding and hesitating are the marks of dishonesty. The wise knower can easily detect them. Moreover, and this is extremely important, these markers will defile the body and corrupt the soul. A defiled and corrupt self is not fit for good living. Put the self in a healthy condition that is conducive to rational thought.

The place of Zara Yacob in the history of philosophy is now firmly established. His corner is clearly the rationalist tradition. The question is: What kind of Rationality did he articulate? This is the topic that I will examine in the next chapter. Siro Contri is quite right, when he argued that,

Zara Yacob drew a rationalistic doctrine,
of an illuminating stamp, in which he
affirms, on the one hand, the infallible

authority of God and of his law, and on the other hand the existence in man of a light of reason which is infallible in it if rightly applied. All authority can and must be judged on the strength of the light of reason.[131]

Chapter VIII

CONCLUSION
The Rationality of the Heart

"In the West, the heart is a symbol of emotions. In the East, the heart gathers into one word a kaleidoscope of forms and colors: the penetrating intelligence ("one understands with one's heart"), moral conscience ("one knows in one's heart what is good and what is evil"), authenticity ("Words reveal the thoughts of one's heart"), the interior axis which polarizes the fragments of the person *("To penetrate a being to its very heart.")*
Claude Sumner *(The Song of Songs, p. 20)*

To the ancient Egyptians, the heart was the seat of reason. The Egyptians mummified the human heart and sucked out the brain. It captured their imagination and stirred their reasoning power to master its inner workings. It is said that hearts were lifted and soaked in wines and herbs, preserved for worship by saints. Aztec priests captured their enemy's hearts, and " offered them to their gods".

The Egyptians were cardocentrists. They considered the brain worthless, whereas they worshipped the heart. The human heart also fascinated the Greek philosophers, Plato and Aristotle. Plato, however, was much more concerned with the soul than he was with the heart. In the Republic, he divides the human soul into three parts, The Rational, the spirited and the desiring part. Privilege of governance is given to Rationality to direct both the spirit and desire. The heart is treated as the seat of desire. Aristotle, his brilliant student parts company from his teacher. As the son of a biologist, accustomed to shrewd observation, he dissected and studied the structure of animal hearts. His *Historia Animalum* and *De Patrbus Animalum* are a wealth of empirical evidence. Since human dissection was illegal at the time, he dissected animals and studied their heart, and discovered that the heart had three chambers, and two vessels. He does not mention the valves. He criticized Plato for considering the heart a cushion. For Aristotle, the heart was the seat of the soul. [132]

The human heart, this efficient and industrious muscular pump, the size of a fist, which beats 100,000 times, and pumps 2000 gallons of blood, through 60,000 miles of blood vessels, and which in a life time will beat more than 2.5 billion times, is also the site of a penetrating intelligence, which deciphers the correct moral path, and originates our moral intelligence. The heart as part of the body is a muscular pump, and as the house of the mind, is an organ of thought. In the body and mind dichotomy that raged in the seventeenth century, with Descartes claim that the body and the mind cannot interact, one possible way by which this dichotomy can be overcome, is the Copernican revolution that Zara Yacob staged, by giving a hint of a resolution. That resolution is his view that the human heart is both part of the body and the mind. As a part of the body it is muscular pump and as the seat of the soul it is the center of thinking, since the creator endowed the heart with a penetrating intelligence. On his view the mind and the body are already interacting in the heart.

> When we use the expression " ratio-nal" we suppose that there is a close relation between rationality and knowledge. Our knowledge has a prepositional structure; beliefs can be represented in the form of statements...for rationality has less to do with the possession of knowledge than with how speaking and acting subjects acquire and use knowledge. (Jurgen Habermas, *The Theory of Communicative Action*, Volume I, p, 8, Beacon Press, 1984

I shall presuppose this conception of rationality, when I argue that the human heart is rational in this particular sense. In the moral-rational sphere, speaking and acting subjects consult the heart before they intervene to take action, motivated by an injustice or simply acting on the calls of a moral and practical vision. The penetrating human intelligence inscribed in the heart as Zara Yacob taught us propels humans to change the world, to transform it by effective moral-rationanl action. The moral-practical thought aiming at changing the sphere of morality is located in the human heart.

Lib, (heart) in Geez is the home of wisdom. It is the fountain of truth. All the feelings percolating there are themselves rational thoughts that can be validated either as true or false. It is the heart that authenticates them.

The brain merely organizes these thoughts as they pertain to the objective world of facts, the subjective world of feelings and the moral-rational world of action. All the thoughts from the three domains percolate in the heart.

Furthermore, Rationality and Reason had been recently sharply distinguished by John Rawls, in his *Political Liberalism*. Rawls understands rationality as a way of planning a life, and by reason he means a way of originating principles in the regulation of our passions and desires. The human heart I would like to propose is rational in both senses. Noesis (Intelligence) according to Zara Yacob is inscribed in the human heart. I think he meant this literally and not metaphorically. Following him, I argue that the intelligence in the human heart enables us both to rationally plan our lives and also originate principles with which to regulate our passions.

A plan of life is articulated in the heart and the relevant principles of reason originate there. In this sense the heart produces intelligent life plans and originates principles of reason to inform our action, to enrich our agency. A plan of life and principles of moral action are functions of noesis, which is located in the human heart. By this account, I would like to modestly propose, the heart is rational as are the feelings that percolate there. Whereas scientific rationality restricts itself to the relationship between means and ends, the heart seeks to make both the means and the ends rational.

When we say that something is from the heart, what we mean is,

(1) The feelings which ground thought are authentic;
(2) That the thought is honest;
(3) That the thought is carefully felt out;
(4) That the agent has distinguished inauthentic thought from authentic one;
(5) That the agent says only what she means;
(6) Finally, the thought provokes moral action; it compels the actor to make decisions.

Understanding the meaning of rationality is a daunting task. This is particularly true for the 21st century, a time of bewildering clashes of cultures and civilizations. The task is complicated further by the challenges of post-modernity which continue to erase rational standards altogether, and threaten us to abandon any quest for rational truth, by arguing that definitions as such are afflicted by the judgments of those in power.[133] I will engage this debate towards in my concluding remarks. For now I will examine the meaning of rationality in the seventeenth century, as Zara Yacob understood it.

Zara Yacob's rationality is clearly and simply

enshrined in the following words, *"To the person who seeks it, truth is immediately revealed. Indeed he who investigates with the pure intelligence set by the creator in the heart of each man and scrutinizes the order and laws of creation will discover the truth."*[134] His follower, Walda Heywat reinforces that thesis, *"A faith without inquiry is not demanded by God and does not befit the nature of a rational creature."*[135] Thirty years earlier one of the greatest rationalists of all time, Rene Descartes wrote, *"We ought never to allow ourselves to be persuaded of the truth of anything unless on the evidence of our reason."*[136] The seventeenth century witnesses the birth of a specific view of rationality that confirms the role of reason as the ultimate power on which any faith must be based. Human errors can be avoided only by the correct use of reason. Interpreting Descartes, Gellner has convincingly argued, *"Liberation from error requires liberation from culture, from example and custom as he calls it. It is this accumulation of complacent, confident conviction, and its acceptance, which leads men into error [...] culture is questionable, Reason is not."*[137] As we recall, Zara Yacob, a fellow rationalist was disdainful of custom and prejudice. He challenges human beings to rely on their own intelligence when they want to believe in anything. Interpreting his teacher's thoughts Walda Heywat argues, *"Hence it is not fitting that we believe in the faith of our fathers before we enquire and come to know that their faith is true. God did not give reason only to our fathers, but to us also and a greater one to them. How can we know that the faith of our fathers is true unless we examine it or understand it from beginning to end?*"[138] Zara Yacob too wanted freedom from custom, or from irrational culture, or a culture that he did not freely choose, but to which he is simply born. He wanted culture to be self-constructed. He distrusted collectively formed customs precisely because they are not constructed through freely developed intelligence, as he so passionately desired. He did not play culture against reason as Gellner's Descartes did. For Zara Yacob, what needs to be dismantled is a culture that is not formed through the use of one's own reason, as his God commanded, and not culture as such. In this sense Descartes and Zara Yacob are different.

In the history of philosophy there continue to prevail different kinds of rationality. Consider the following paradigmatic ones. The first classical model is Aristotle's. For Aristotle, rationality is a function of the activity of the soul. The rational person is one who works on the soul by subjecting desire to reason at all times. Happy is the individual who knows that she has a soul and that the different parts of the soul, particularly the nonrational parts, must be guided by the principle of excellence, and excellence is rationality.[139] Following him, Kant, the modernist conceives of the rational person, as moral, and the moral person, as one who subjects desire to guidance by the categorical imperative of practical reason.[140] She must subject desire willingly or else the action would not be worthy of morality, if the agent feels coerced. The agent must freely choose subjection to the imperatives of practical reason, convinced by the reasonableness of the choice. Otherwise, her choice is irrational and non-moral. In *Political Liberalism*, the modern rationalist, John Rawls defends Rationality as goodness. He writes,

> *This idea supposes that the members of a democratic society have, at least in an intuitive way, a rational plan of life in the light of which they schedule their various resources (including those of mind and body, time and energy) so as to pursue their conceptions of the good over a complete life, if not in the most rational, then at least in a sensible (or satisfactory), way […] goodness as rationality provides part of a framework serving two main roles: first, it helps us to identify a workable list of goods and second, relying on a index of these goods, it enables us both to specify the aims (or motivation) of the parties in the original position and to explain why those aims (or motivation) are rational.* [141]

Recently Gellner, in *Reason and Culture*, has insightfully argued that in modernity rationality has become a way of life. Summarizing a Cartesian view of rationality, he writes,

> *A rational person is methodical and precise. He is tidy and orderly, above all in thought. He does not raise his voice, his tone, is steady and equal; that goes for his feelings as well as his voice. He separates all separable issues, and deals with them one at a time. By so doing, he avoids muddling up issues and conflating dis-*

> *tinct criteria [...] He methodically aug-*
> *ments his capital, cognitive as well as*
> *financial. He ploughs back his profits*
> *rather than turning them into pleasure,*
> *power, or status.*[142]

This is for the most part the dominant model of rationality in the industrialized world. Gellner captures the mood of modernity so accurately. For Gellner, though, it is Hume the advocate of passion to which reason is a slave that has a superior explanatory power. As Gellner puts the matter, *"The impotence of Reason is itself an independent truth of reason. Hume showed that the clear and distinct data did not permit a cogent inference to the kind of world we in fact inhabit and manipulate."*[143] He is not endorsing any unreason as an alternative to reason, but simply arguing that the modern world is neither, and that individuals are rapidly loosing a sense of identity. The modern has become destabilized. Thus the post-modern challenge, which Gellner does not engage as extensively as Calvin Schrag does in *The Resources of Rationality*.

In this important work, Schrag develops a new model of rationality that he calls *"the transversal rationality of praxis"*. The transversal model defends reason against the attacks of post-modernity. He writes, *"Transversality effects a unification and integration, a communication across differences, that does not congeal into a seamless solidarity or locus of coincidence. It brings the various viewpoints lying across the landscape of the remembered past into a communicative situation that recognizes the in-*

tegrity of particularity and the play of diversity"[144]
On this view, disputes between the Arabs and the
Jews, Indians and Pakistanis, Irish and English,
and many other kinds, can be resolved by foster-
ing a respectful respect of the other's views, of other
doxas. Schrag put it well. *"The rationality of such
negotiations resides in an understanding of the particular traditions in which each of the parties are situ-
ated and in a recognition of the need to make accom-
modations and adjustments through a transversal
movement of responding to that which is at once other
and alien."*[145] This particular kind of rationality
seeks to respond the post-modern challenge that
has jettisoned completely the virtue of rationality
as an ideal for humanity, contending that rationality allocates power and privilege vertically, and
that it is the tool that the west used to subjugate
the non-west, and furthermore, it is disrespectful
of Doxas, the ordinary persons power of partici-
pating in discourse. For all these reasons the post-
modernists are dead set against rationality.

With a different tone Alistair Macintyre has
also sought to show the historicity and traditional
boundedness of rationality, thereby correcting the
excesses of the claims of some of Enlightenment
thinkers. Rationality, Macintyre forcefully argued,
is intimately wedded to tradition and history. It is
illusory to think that rationality is homeless-
bound by nothing except the commitment to truth,
from a neutral standpoint. Macintyre writes,

> *So we are still confronted by the claims
> to our rational allegiance of the rival*

> *traditions whose histories I have nar-
> rated, and indeed, depending upon where
> and how we raise the questions about
> justice and practical rationality, by a
> number of other such traditions. We have
> learned that we cannot ask and answer
> those questions from a standpoint exter-
> nal to all tradition, that the resources of
> adequate rationality are made available
> to us only in and through traditions. How
> then are we to confront those questions?
> To what account of practical rational-
> ity and of justice do we owe our assent?
> How we in fact answer these latter ques-
> tions, we now have to notice, will de-
> pend in key part upon what the lan-
> guage is which we share with those to-
> gether with whom we ask them ques-
> tions and to what point the history of
> our own linguistic community has
> brought us.*[146]

Rationality for Macintyre belongs to cultures, traditions, customs and examples, contra Descartes
and Zara Yacob, who attempted to free rationality from history and tradition, and make it an attribute given by the transcendent, who himself is
outside history and time. The transcendent allocates powers to the individual as an individual and
not as a member of tradition and custom. It is the
individual's intelligence and moral power that is
appealed to when correct decisions are expected.
Zara Yacob in particular is unsparing in his criti-
cisms and analyses of traditions and customs. Not
only that, Zara Yacob's vision of rationality is radi-

cally different even from that of Descartes, his spiritual mate.

Rationality for Zara Yacob is an activity of the human heart blessed by a moral intelligence that is given to all human beings, should they choose to make use of this extraordinary gift. Having a gift and actually using it are of course two different things, but for those who would like to do the morally right thing, the heart is ready to help them perform the important task of performing in a morally worthy manner. Such individuals do not have to go beyond consulting their heart when they agonize over their decisions, over their choices and over their dreams of seeking to be exceptional human beings. In almost every other page of the Treatises, both Zara Yacob and Walda Heywat continue to refer to the human heart as the ultimate place of profound thought. In none of the modalities of rationality, that I briefly summarized, is the human heart acknowledged as the source of thought. The heart is subtly treated as the place of meandering emotions and fickle feelings, or else, it is simply ignored. Zara Yacob was the first to reconfigure rationality, by reordering the relationship between the brain and the heart. The brain for him is a processing machine and nothing more beyond that. The heart is the home of thought. The brain's function is not the production of thought, as the rationality of Descartes assumed. The production of thought is an activity of the heart. The heart, however, does not do this alone. The task it too overwhelming for the heart. There is another, power, which aids the heart to perform its function. The transcendent responds to the hearts desire to communicate and defend the truth. The heart desires, and the force inside it, discloses itself during the intense moments of searching (*Hassasa*) and meditating (*Hatata*). The thinking heart pressured by the pangs of existence, responding to injustices in the world, cries out for help, and realizing its contingency, and the transcendent responds with generous action. Zara Yacob writes:

> *O my Lord and creator who endowed me with reason, make me intelligent, reveal to me your hidden wisdom. Keep my eyes open lest they slumber until the moment of death. Your hands made me and molded me; render me intelligent that I may know your precepts [...] while I was praying in such and similar ways, one day I said to myself in my own thought: Whom am I praying to or is there a God who listens to me. At this thought I was invaded by a dreadful sadness and I said: In vain have I kept my own heart pure.*[147]

This paragraph is an eloquent testimony to the importance that the philosopher attached to reaching out beyond himself to the depth of the heart to be graced with the wisdom of the creator. All his dreams emanate not in the mechanical sound of the brain but in the turbulent murmur of the heart, disturbed by thought, hit by anxiety, sometimes afflicted by hopelessness, desperately inviting the transcendent to visit, and to place wisdom to humble the contingent truth that is in our heart.

Without the guidance provided by the one who truly knows all that we have is what is in our hearts, half-baked truths, lies, envies and jealousies typical of the human condition. These vices can only be cured when we look for God, when we meditate about his greatness, and his vast knowledge. Thanking the transcendent is also thinking, philosophizing, ascending to the summit of infinity, wisdom and absolute knowledge. Zara Yacob unfailingly thanked the transcendent. Thanking is thinking. Thanking is a moral exercise of the cultivation of the virtue of modesty. The philosopher converses with the transcendent both to appeal to him when he is at a loss, and afterwards, as a recipient of wisdom. He thanks God for the wisdom and prays to him for help. Thanking is an act of rejoicing. Rejoicing is thanking, and thanking is thinking. Zara Yacob believed in God as hard as iron.

The philosopher is not ashamed to openly declare the love, iron like faith. Every page in the *Treatise* is suffused with this rational love. All his sentences begin and end with the mention of God. This in not accidental. It is deliberate, because the philosopher is carrying this God in the interiors of his heart, he feels him, he thinks him. He cries out for Him. He worships Him. He thanks Him again and again. We, his readers, are invited to witness this love, through his eloquent writing, and in his prayers.

Contra and Schrag Macintyre, the children of modernity and advocates of scientific rationality, who attempt to ground rationality in tradition and customs, Zara Yacob seeks to free rationality from tradition, and locality. For him there is a universal God who created all human beings as equals. All of us are made of the same fabric. Although, we do not speak the same language, all of us are capable of extending our moral imagination to understand the needs and passions of the so-called "others". There is no need for techniques of understanding "others", as if they are made of a different fabric. It does not require much to understand the languages of despair and hunger. All that we need to do is decide how the hungry must feel, and what our duties are to end that condition, particularly when we are sitting on wealth and power that we do not really need, apart from the status and power that accompany that condition, and how it sometimes blinds our vision, and crowds our ears with flattery and praise. None of this requires transversality to understand. We are already in possession of intelligence by with we can identify our duties and obligations. All that we need to do is wake up the sluggish self.

What we should fear the most is the other in us: the vain, selfish, and self-regarding other. The "other" outside will be taken care of by the just transcendent. The frightening other is us, when we become overwhelmed by our projects, our plans, our careers, at the expense of all those individuals who can benefit from our attention, our kindness and care. However, the challenging task is the death of the morally unmotivated other, the other in us. That other needs to be cured, and be replaced by a vigilant, morally attentive, caring other, who listens to the voice of the heart. The cultivation of the moral self is one of the perennial themes of moral philosophy. For millennia some philosophers have attempted to cultivate a moral citizen. Others like the philosopher Thomas Hobbes, who is chief among them, has argued that there is no such self. The real self is selfish and brutish, whose vices only the law can silence. Zara Yacob too does not have much regard for the natural self, and yet he thinks that this selfish self can be cured by the rationality of the heart, if it dutifully prays to the transcendent. The decision to have a prayerful attitude toward life is the beginning of the healing process. Without that initial decision nothing can be accomplished. The broken self of modernity suffers from this un-prayerful attitude. The rationality of the heart can enable the broken self to mend its heart.

To say that the heart is rational is not to assume that feeling is superior to intellect, as we have sloppily come to infest our language. The theorists of negritude are therefore profoundly mistaken to draw the conclusion that some individuals feel and others think, and that Africans feel and Europeans think. The rationality of the heart does not imply any of this. The heart is the seat of thinking for all of us and thought is suffused with feeling.

Therefore, to think is to feel. Thought itself is feeling. And there can be no thought devoid of feeling. A thought that is devoid of feeling is precisely what makes an "other" to us. Our thought lacks a focus, a moral purpose. It is when that happens that the empty and inattentive other takes hold of our character. At that nodal point we become wedded to our own ego. We exist only for us. Anyone else becomes a subordinate, and a necessary object for our projects. We exploit others without shame, without moral thought. We naturalize our actions as facets of the human condition and some modern disciplines even justify us.

The death of morality is thus officially sanctioned. This death however, can be obviated if moral philosophy attends to it, sufficiently early. The rationality of the heart is superior to the other kinds that I summarized earlier, because it has put compassion and the recognition of our finitude as central elements of thought. Zara Yacob and Walda Heywat are right for arguing that true thinking is transcendental, in the sense that considering the inherent sluggishness of humans, motivating us to do the right is going to require a force much stronger than us. Not once does Zara Yacob fail to acknowledge his limitations. He says again and again that he is weak, lazy and that he needs help. So he searches for the transcendent, meditates on His greatness, and asks Him to make him intelligent. He hopes and patiently waits for the transcendent to reveal himself. When He is thus revealed, he sings His praises, and thanks Him. Zara Yacob writes,

> The work of God is splendid and the thought of him whose wisdom is ineffable is deep indeed. How then can man who is small and poor lie by saying, 'I am sent by God to reveal to men his wisdom and his justice? But man reveals to

*us nothing but vain and contemptible
things, or things whose nature is by far
inferior to the reason that the creator gave
us that we may understand his greatness. And I said: I am little and poor in
your sight, O Lord; make me understand
what I should know about you, that I
may admire your greatness and praise
you everyday with a new praise.*[148]

There is no self-flagellation here. It is genuine
humility. He is prayerfully appealing to God to
complete his intelligence, to grant him wisdom.
He is not asking the transcendent to think for
him or to choose for him. His request is subtle; he
hopes that he will be given the necessary intelligence by which he will decide for himself. The
philosopher does not defer the power to think to
the transcendent. He insists on retaining that
power, exactly as the transcendent intended. He
only wants to learn the way of the transcendent;
the way of thought, realizing that human thought
is incomplete and dependent. He and Descartes
are one in their recognition of human finitude, as
I demonstrated in chapter one. Walda Heywat is
equally emphatic about his finitude, when he
writes, *"Moreover, I write this book to offend the faithful, but to direct the wise and the intelligent towards
an inquiry which will enable them to search for and
find truth; for to examine anything that is good is
wisdom and praise our creator who gave us a rational soul and intelligence with which we may enquire about him."*[149] Again exactly like his teacher,
he beseeches the transcendental to give him the

power of thought, so as to unravel truth. He adds, "*Reason teaches me that my soul is created rational that it may know its creator, praise him, thank him at all times, and serve [him] according to that service that the creator destined for it, investigate and understand his will in all the things it does, worship him without deceit as long as it will be in this life and in this body.*"[150] He too thanks the creator, and praises His name. He writes movingly, "*I do not say to you do not tempt me, but make me accept the fight and be patient, as becomes your rational creature if it pleases you to tempt it: uphold me, lest I falter or repudiate you in any way; make me praise you always, when you do good to me with your blessing, when you tempt me with your holy will; you are indeed my Lord and my God before centuries and for all centuries.*"[151] These two philosophers' commitment to the transcendent is as powerful as David's in the *Psalms*. The *Psalms* of David happen to be their model of love, devotion, thankfulness and prayer to the transcendent. They are powerful models for believers, and perhaps tempting examples for non-believers.

The rationality of the heart (RH) does precisely attempt to solve human problems through the mediation of the heart, the heart as the dwelling place of thought; and I am enormously grateful to Zara Yacob for leaving such a powerful vehicle of thought that I am convinced would be in service of modernity, since modernity is desperately in need of the language of the heart. I must add, however, that I am essentially following the spirit of Zara Yacob's celebration of the heart. The rest is my own interpretation of the functions of the heart. I use Zara Yacob only as a stepping ladder. I start with an interpretation of Zara Yacob's views of the matter, as I understand it. I then proceed to defend the thesis that feeling actually grounds thought, and that feeling itself is a profound modality of meditation, a form of thought, and thought itself is mediated through feeling.

One way of celebrating the virtues, not to say the distinctiveness of the Rationality of the Heart (RH), is to compare it to Scientific Rationality (SR). I will begin with a detailed discussion of SR in the first section, and then proceed to contrast it with RH, in the second section.

The meaning of Rationality has puzzled a long line of prominent thinkers, Claude Sumner among them. According to Sumner, Zara Yacob had been referred to as the first African rationalist in many complex senses. Zara Yacob's rationality is centered on "the light of the intellect"; it is anchored upon human reason and God's infinite wisdom.

SR is the dominant form of thought in the western world, and the non-western world seems to be rapidly racing to embrace it. Before proceeding to compare these rationalities, I would first like to clearly articulate the nature of SR. For the most part SR is exclusively focused on meeting the economical and psychological needs of the individual. On this view rational is the individual who articulates his individual needs and then devices the appropriate means with which to satisfy them. The articulated ends must fit the chosen means perfectly. Otherwise, the action is irrational. Moreover, the rational individual is not expected to take the needs of others into account, unless recognizing and satisfying their needs is crucial for the satisfaction of her own life plan.

John Rawls writes:

> *Reasonable and rational agents are normally the units of responsibility in political and social life and may be charged with violations of reasonable principles and standards. The rational is however, a distinct idea from the reasonable and applies to a single, unified agent (either an individual or corporate person with the powers of judgment and deliberation in seeking ends and interests peculiarly its own…what rational agents lack is the particular form of moral sensibility that underlies the desire to engage in fair cooperation as such, and to do so on terms that others as equals might reasonably be expected to endorse.*[152]

Clearly SR which is also motivated by the kind of Rationality that Rawls described is precisely, as I will argue below, that compels me to defend RH, which is propelled not only by principles but also by compassion, as a better vehicle of thought. One of the disturbing limits of SR is that it is too self-centered. The need to think about undesirable consequences of our actions, consequences to human life, to the environment, just to mention two glaring examples, is not taken into account. The self is so self-regarding that it does not make any effort to weigh its claim against another. In contrast, RH is remarkably sensitive to other people's claims, to the consequences for the God created human creatures, and the natural world that we cannot blindly violate. SR disregards norms and values. RH is suffused by these concerns. SR is an example of a disinterested quest for Justice, should justice affect the mood of the person. RH is an intensely and passionately engaged human heart, which wants to obviate the occurrence of justice of ever surfacing in the purified human heart. This is of course what the rational person has to consciously work on-studiously and habitually. It is a self-conscious practice of cultivating new habits of the heart. RH attempts to overthrow the weight of tradition. It goes in the opposite direction that Macintyre moves with his questionable notion of contested rationalities, when he argues:

> *Traditions fail the Cartesian test of beginning from unassailable evident truths; not only do they begin from contingent Traditions also fail the Hegelian test of showing that their goal is some form of rational state which they share with all other movements of thought. Traditions are always and radically to some degree local, informed by particularities of language and social and natural environment, inhabited by Greeks or by citizens of Roman Africa or medieval Persia or by eighteenth century Scots, who stubbornly refuse to be or become vehicles of the self-realization of Geist.*[153]

He is right that coercing traditions and their rationalities to a size fit all notion of Geist under which they will be subsumed would result in the loss of culturally nuanced systems of justification and loss of individuality. The loss of individuality had led the able Beninois philosopher, Paulin Hountondji to bitterly complain that:

> I start from the assumption that values are no one's property, that no intrinsic necessity lies behind their distribution across various civilizations or their changing relative importance; for instance, if science is today more spectacularly developed in Europe than in Africa, this is due not to the specific and unique qualities of the white race but to a particularly favorable set of circumstances. This historical accident does not make science an essentially European value—any more than syphilis, introduced into Amerindian societies by the first visitors from the old World, is an essentially European disease. Cultural values are like venereal diseases: they flourish here and there, develop in one place rather than another according to whether the environment is more or less favorable; but this purely historical accident cannot justify any claim to ownership or, for that matter, to immunity.[154]

Hountondji is a proponent of SR, which he hopes would be implanted in the African soil, convinced that Africa's ills can be changed only by a shift in the gaze of thought, away from ethnophilosphy and unanimism and toward the objectivity of Science, and with it the scientification of thought, hence the obsession with SR. There are good reasons for admiring some of the features of SR, that it is unburdened by artificial unanimity, allows the dissemination of individual opinions, seeks to maximize neutrality and objectivity of decisions, and most importantly encourages the positive intrusion of technological facilities to ease the pains of African everyday life. Hountondji is right when he argues that, " *Science is generated by discussion and thrives on it. If we want science in Africa, we must create in the continent a human environment in which and by which the most diverse problems can be freely debated and in which these discussions can be no less freely recorded and disseminated, thanks to the written word, to be submitted to the appreciation of all and transmitted to future generations. These, I am sure, will do much better than we have.* "[55] The statement is adequate but it does not help the reader what science means in this ambiguous context, is it medical science or technological science that he has in mind. If the latter, then one would have to carefully screen the kinds of technology that are appropriate for the African experience. Africans have learned bitterly that not all technology is appropriate for Africa. One has to be selective; this is particularly true of medical science. There are certain diseases that are best handled by traditional medication, and others that are best handled by advanced western techniques. Every intervention to the African body has to respect African experience and African solutions. Hountondji ignores this need for specific situations, whereas Kwame Gyekye is right in a sense that Hountondji is not, when he advocates that, *"Our historical knowledge of how the results of cultural encounter occur seems to suggest that what is needed is, not the transfer or transplant of technology: a perception of method that features the active, adroit, and purposeful imitative and participation of the recipients in the pursuit and acquisition of a technology of foreign production"*[156] Hountondji does not even pay lip service to them.

Anthony Appiah is even subtler and convincing in pointing out the inadequacy of SR and technological prowess, when he writes, *" There is a similar set of difficulties with Weber's account of rationalization. In The Protestant Ethic and the Spirit of Capitalism, Weber wrote, ' If this essay makes any contribution at all, may it be to bring out the complexity of the only superficially simple concept of the rational'. But we may be tempted to ask whether our understanding of the genuine complexities of the historical developments of the last few centuries of social, religious, economic, and political history of Western Europe is truly deepened by making use of a concept of rationalization that brings together a supposed increase in means-end calculation (instrumental rationality); a decline to appeal to "mysterious, incalculable forces" and a correlative increasing confidence in calculation (disenchantment or intellectualization); and the growth of "value rationality," which means something like an increasing focus on maximizing a narrow range of ultimate goals."*[157]

Appiah is correctly noting the inherent limitations of this highly rationalized theory of reason, and the way it is seeping into the fabric of

modern life in Africa. Modernity in Africa is being rapidly rationalized, but I think this decision
is a mistaken one. To be sure, the rich and powerful are using [SR] for their ends. Some of the rich-
est men in the world are now in Africa; shamelessly depleting African resources; enriching
themselves on the backs of the poor; subjecting
six year olds to psychological and physical abuse;
sending their children to the most expensive uni-
versities in the west; when they can they place
their own children in unearned positions of power
and financial comfort. Merit is a play thing of the
scientific rationalists, indifference to suffering is
a way of life, the struggle of the fittest is an ideology, going to church and praying is a habit without the heart. The church in Africa is the rich
man's church. It is there to justify the begetting of
wealth by any means necessary, since the rich and
powerful believe that God helps only those who
cannot help themselves. It is widely believed that
the poor are poor because they cannot help themselves, that they are irrational, that they do not
plan well. These are the myths of SR that have
been used as weapons of the rich.

RH has the potential to redeem us all from
ourselves, from the slumber of our sleep, our cal-
lousness and indifference. These are turbulent
times. Indifference is the signifier of the age. Game
playing is the name of human relations. We play
people. We like to say play him this way. Make
sure that you play her that way is the other side of
the coin. We do this without shame. We even like
to say-sadly-do not be emotional. Be reasonable.
Note the way we separate emotion from reason.

Worse still, we always make sure that our decisions are rational, to the extent that we remove our passions, the center of emotion from guiding our decision. Just imagine the persons that we encounter daily; those who devotedly clean our offices, those who silently man our elevators, those who look after our children when we work away long ours, those who smilingly serve us at restaurants. We treat them indifferently. We say to ourselves they are doing their job, performing a task for which they are being paid. Yet, we know that most of these jobs are inadequately paid, but are miserable, insulting. They deaden the nerves. They harden and embitter the people who perform them. Study after study has documented this. To respond to these facts of modern life requires not only the calculative services of SR but also more fundamentally the participation of the human heart, and that is how RH enters the picture, to protect us against ourselves. When we listen to the heart-the sit of thought - we will not suffer from the subtle assaults of thoughtlessness in the peculiar form of indifference and internalized cruelty. We have become accustomed not to respond to these conditions, as Zara Yacob and Walda Heywat demand from our hearts. We conclude too quickly that these individuals are fated to live this way, and that the best that SR enables us to do for them, is at least employ them. Even that is not looked at as a right that these human beings have.

Indifference and cruelty, we have been told by a long line of philosophers (Plato, Aristotle, Kant and Hobbes) and novelists (Dostoyevsky) are natural emotions, and that there is very little that we can do to change them. The philosophers and novelists seem to be right if we evaluate the proposition by the yardstick of human practices over a long period of human history. A proposition however is not only a descriptive affirmation of a practice, but also a symbolic, however, mythical the symbol is, of possibility, and a new way of leading our lives against the background of what we know about human beings. The symbolic possibility challenges human beings by signaling to them that they can be other than what they have become.

Nothing can change us if we are dogmatically convinced that there is very little that we can do to change the world that constantly bombards us with pessimistic diagnoses of the human condition. SR does not help very much when all that it teaches us the exact calculation of our interests, with very little encouragement to come out of the cocoon of comfort and docility. If we decide to pay attention to the heart, first and foremost, we will be flooded with the warmth and the love that we immediately feel for our fellow human beings. The heart will force us to pay attention to all those who labor silently. A smile at the busy cashier, a conversation with the garbage keeper, a hug of the starving child, a hefty wage for the care taker, a place in our heart for those who cannot see a doctor, a genuine concern for the twelve years old who was raped on day light, become our daily preoccupations. We do not do them reluctantly as Kant sometimes preaches. We do them lovingly and willingly because we are thinking through our heart, not because we are enforcing the principles of moral reason, like many proficient bureaucrats. To think is not merely to be stimulated by moral reason. Thinking is genuinely affected by pain in the world. It is an exercise in going out of the enclosed space of self-obsession to embrace another human being. Thinking in this sense is an activity of the heart. To argue that the call to action that the thinking heart stimulates is rational is not to denigrate the role of moral principles. In a very subtle sense the principles of reason are not produced by the mind but are generated by the activity of the heart. Principles are the vehicles of the thought that takes place in the heart itself, and which the brain organizes. Principles are the mediations of thought. This is particularly true of moral thought, which is the sphere to which I am applying RH.

Thinking invites us to get in touch with our hearts. Getting in touch with our hearts concretely means letting us experience the mystery of being. It also means opening us to the disclosure of being's invitation to see, hear and touch. All our senses are awakened to the presence of the reflective presence. The heart responds to the calls of a raped child, a starved family, an abandoned wife, unfulfilled husband, a celebration of a modest wedding, a funeral service of someone who you met and loved instantly. Thinking accompanied by joy and heavy sadness takes place in the interiors of the human heart. It is when we respond to the calls of life that one could surmise that we are thinking.

Appendix

The Debates over the Authenticity over Zara Yacob's *Treatise*

The debates over the *Treatise* have over whelmed Claude Sumner and his opponents for a few years. I would first to summarize the arguments and then provide my position. Sumner is the very best voice defending the thesis that the author of the *Hatatas* is none other than Zara Yacob himself. As Sumner puts it:

> Some go further and argue that what we take as Zara Yacob's writing is not actually his but of an Italian Capuchin Giustô d''Urbino. Giusto d'Urbino, an Italian monk who lived in Ethiopia in the 19th century is said to have bought the manuscript of Zara Yacob and Welde Hiywot and sent the manuscript back to Antoine d'Abbadie in Paris. Some have picked

this fact and preferred to conclude that the author of the two manuscripts is Giusto d'Urbino himself.

He continues:

True. But I do have some evidence against this argument. The first argument is that Giusto d'Urbino himself clearly indicated that the manuscripts are not of his own. And I do not see any reason why a European thinker of such caliber produces such a refined philosophical work and at the end ascribes it to some 'Ethiopian Philosopher' that never existed. I could not possibly think of any not to believe Giusto d'Urbino himself who tells us clearly that he bought the manuscripts.

Further:

The second argument is linguistic in nature. Here we should note that Giusto d Urbino, though he did manage to learn Ge'ez, was in no position to write such a manuscript. Still some accept the fact that Giusto d'Urbino could have dictated his ideas to an Ethiopian scribe who could have captured his ideas in refined Ge'ez. Yes, even the argument does not hold true. You see there is a manuscript-Les Soirees de Carthage de Francois Bourgade. Both Giusto d'Urbino and his Ethioiopian Scribe write this manuscript. The first part is written by Giusto d'Urbino himself and the second part by his clerk. A thorough study of these writings by a prominent instructor of Ge'ez literature at Addis Ababa University, Alemayehu Moges, has clearly indicated that, primarily, Giusto d"Urbino's writing in Ge'ez is full of mistakes. The scribe's writing was found to be free of errors but the type of languages used by Giusto d'Urbino scribe and the language of Zara Yacob were completely different. This clearly shows that neither Giusto d'Urbino's scribe and the language of Zara Yacob were completely different. This clearly shows that neither Giusto d'Urbino nor his scribe could have possibly been the author of the manuscript that I strongly insist to be of Zara Yacob.[158]

End Notes

1. Sumner, *Ethiopian Philosophy*, VOL I. P 369.
2. Ibid. P 26.
3. Ibid. P 110.
4. Claude Sumner, *Classical Ethiopian Philosophy*, p, 106.
5. Ibid. P 111.
6. Ibid, p, 339.
7. Claude Sumner, Classical Ethiopian Philosophy, PP, 51-52.
8. Ibid, P, 75.
9. For an explication of the way ideas and views become hegemonic see Teodros Kiros, *Moral Philosophy and Development*, Columbus: Ohio University Press, 1985.
10. Ibid, p, 83.
11. Ibid, p, 91.
12. Ibid, p, 91.
13. Kwame Gyekye, *Tradition and Modernity: Philosophical Reflections on the African Experience*, Oxford: Oxford University press, 1997 P 217.
14. Claude Sumner, *Classical Ethiopian Philosophy*, p, 234.
15. Ibid. P 236.
16. Ibid. P 236. I have quoted this passage earlier in a different context. I have requited many such important passages, because the new contexts and arguments demanded the passages. I aplologize for the redundance, but I discovered that readability was considerably improved by such method.
17. Ibid. P 238.
18. Ibid. P 239.
19. Ibid. P 238.
20. Ibid. P 248.
21. Ibid. P 238.
22. Ibid. P 244-245.
23. *The Itinerary of Jeromino Lobo*, The Haklutt Society. London, 1984, p.154.)
24. Ibid, p.157.
25. Charles F.Rez, (H.F. & G. Witherby, 1929, p.301)
26. Lobo. *Itinerary*, P.159.
27. Ibid, p, 169.

28. *Prutsky's* Travels in Ethiopia and Other countries, Second Series No 174, The Halkutt Society, 1991, P, 276.
29. The *Lost Empire* (Phillip Caramon, University of Notre dame Press, 1985) p, 123.
30. Ibid. P, 52.
31. Ibid, P, 143.
32. Ibid, P, 145.
33. Ibid, P, 148.
34. Donald Levine, *Wax and Gold* (The University of Chicago Press, 1965) pp, 268-269.
35. Claude Sumner, *Classical Ethiopian Philosophy*, Los Angeles: Adey Publishers, 1994,
36. Ibid, p, 243.
37. Rene Descartes, *Meditations on First Philosophy*, Cambridge: Hacket Publishing Company, 1993. P, 30
38. Claude Sumner, *Classical Ethiopian Philosophy*, p, 234
39. Ibid, p232.
40. Ibid, P234.
41. Ibid, PP. 234-235.
42. Ibid, PP. 243-244.
43. Ibid, P, 246.
44. Rene Descartes, *Meditations on First Philosophy*, Hacket Publishing Company, 1999.
45. Ibid, P, 28.
46. Ibid, p, 30.
47. Ibid, p, 41.
48. Ibid, p, 57.
49. Ibid, p, 58.
50. *Classical Ethiopian Philosophy*, P, 241.
51. Descartes, *Meditations On First Philosophy*. The word faith is not used in the meditations directly. The spirit of the argument is scattered through out the meditations, from which I extracted a few possible arguments about faith.
52. Claude Sumner, Classical Ethiopian *Philosophy*, PP. 240-241.
53. *Descartes, Meditations on First Philosophy, p, 19.*
54. *Ibid, p, 30.*
55. *Ibid, p, 230-231*
56. *Claude Sumner, Classical Ethiopian Philosophy, p, 242.*
57. *Ibid, p, 42.*

58. *Ibid, p, 243.*
59. *Ibid, p, 245.*
60. *Ibid, p.246.*
61. *Ibid, p, 246.*
62. *Ibid, p, 233.*
63. *Ibid, p, 234.*
64. *Ibid, p, 234.*
65. *Ibid, p, 235.*
66. *Ibid, p, 236.*
67. *Ibid, p, 236.*
68. *Ibid, p, 237.*
69. *Ibid, pp, 237-238*
70. *Ibid, p, 239.*
71. *Ibid, p, 240.*
72. *Ibid., p, 241.*
73. *Ibid, p, 241.*
74. *Ibid, p, 235.*
75. *Ibid, p, 235.*
76. *Martin Oswald (translator) Nicomachean Ethics, Library of Liberal Arts, Prentice Hall, 1962. See book 2, where Aristotle a theory of moral virtue as habit. See also, Kwame Gyekye, The Akan Conceptual Scheme, and Philadelphia: Temple University Press, 1987. Chapters 9 and 10 are convincing articulations of moral virtue as habit. Of course Aristotle has developed a systematic program of cultivation this virtue as a function of practical reason.*
77. *Classical Ethiopian Philosophy, p, 235.*
78. *Ibid, p, 235.*
79. *Ibid, p, 248.*
80. *Ibid, p, 248.*
81. *Ibid, p, 240.*
82. *Ibid, p, 236.*
83. *Ibid, p, 236.*
84. *Ibid, 237.*
85. *Ibid, 242.*
86. *Ibid, 244.*
87. *Ibid, p, 243.*
88. *Ibid, p, 243.*
89. *Ibid, p, 245.*
90. *Ibid, p, 247.*

91. *Ibid, p, 246.*
92. *Martin Heidegger, Discourse on Thinking, and New York: Harper and Row publishers, 1966, p, 55.*
93. *Ibid, p, 89.*
94. *Ibid, p, 90.*
95. *Claude Sumner, Classical Ethiopian Philosophy, p, 246.*
96. *Ibid, p, 254.*
97. *Ibid, p, 255.*
98. *Ibid, p, 256.*
99. *Ibid, 259.*
100. *Ibid, 261.*
101. *Ibid, 265.*
102. *Ibid, PP, 267-269.*
103. *Ibid, p, 270.*
104. *Ibid. P 271.*
105. *Ibid. P 273.*
106. *Ibid. P 273.*
107. *Ibid, 274.*
108. *Ibid, p, 279.*
109. *Ibid, p, 248.*
110. *Ibid, p, 276.*
111. *Ibid. P, 278.*
112. *Ibid. P, 278.*
113. *Ibid. P, 282.*
114. *Ibid. P, 283.*
115. *Niccolo Machiavelli, The Prince,*
116. *Claude Sumner, Classical Ethiopian Philosophy, p, 285.*
117. *Ibid, p, 287.*
118. *Ibid, p, 287.*
119. *These are the words of Anthony Appiah, from his preface to Classical Ethiopian Philosophy.*
120. *Paulin J. Hountondji, African Philosophy: Myth and Reality, Bloomington: Indiana University Press, 1996, pp 55-56.*
121. *Ibid, viii.*
122. *See the fascinating debates and dialogues among the stars philosophizing on Africa in Teodros Kiros (Ed) Explorations in African Political Thought: Identity, Community, Ethics (New York: Routledge, 2001)*
123. *Immanuel Kant, Foundations of the Metaphysics of Mor-*

End Notes

als, NJ: Library of Liberal Arts (Ed. Lewis White Beck)
1995, p, 83.

124. *Claude Sumner, Classical Ethiopian Philosophy, p, 236.*
125. *Kwasi Wiredu, Cultural Universals and Particulars, P, 63.*
126. *Paulin Hountondji, African Philosophy: Myth and Reality, P, 86.*
127. *Aristotle, Nicomachean Ethics (translated by Martin Oswald) Englewood Cliffs: NJ, Library of Liberal Arts, 1962, 288.*
128. *Ibid, p, 294.*
129. *Ibid. P, 289.*
130. *Claude Sumner, Classical Ethiopian Philosophy, p, 232.*
131.
132. Andrea Marcogliese, *The Pulse of Generations: Plato, Aristotle, and "Hippocrates" on the Heart*, , 1995, Classics, May 7,1995.
133. Calvin O.Schrag, *The Resources of Rationality, A Response to the Postmodern Challenge*, Bloomington: Indiana University Press, 1992. See Chapter for challenging defenses of reason. See also my own book, *Self-Construction and The Formation of Human Values: Truth, Language and Desire*, Connecticut: Praeger,2001.
134. Claude Sumner, *Classical Ethiopian Philosophy*, p,236.
135. Ibid, p, 259.
136. Rene Descartes, *Discourse on Method*, part IV (first published 1637)
137. Ernest Gellner, *Reason and Culture: New perspectives on the past*, Oxford: Blackwell, 1992, p, 3.
138. Claude Sumner, *Classical Ethiopian Philosophy*, p,258.
139. Aristotle, *Nichomachean Ethics*, p, 17.
140. Immanuel Kant, *Foundations of the Metaphysics of Morals*, second section.
141. John Rawls, *Political Liberalism*, Columbia University Press, 1993, pp, 177-178.
142. Ernest Gellner, *Reason and Culture*, pp, 136-137.
143. Ibid, p, 179.
144. Calvin o. Schrag, *The Resources of Rationality: A Response to the Postmodern Challenge*, Bloomington: Indiana University Press, 1992,p, 154.

145. Ibid. P 170.
146. Alistair Macintyre, *Whose Justice? Which Rationality,* Notre Dame: University of Notre Press, 1988, P, 369.
147. Claude Sumner, *Classical Ethiopian Philosophy,* pp, 232-233.
148. Ibid. P 246.
149. Ibid. P 258.
150. Ibid. P 260.
151. Ibid. P 265.
152. John Rawls, *Political Liberalism,* p, 50.
153. Alasdair Macintyre, *Whose Justice? Which Rationality,* P, 361
154. Paulin Hountondji, *African Philosophy,* p, 177.
155. Ibid, p, 46.
156. Kwame Gyekye, *Tradition and Modernity,* p, 285.
157. Anthony Appiah, *In My Father's House,* p, 147.
158. Claude Sumner, *Liber Amicorum,* (Forthcoming).